Legal Almanac Series No. 86

PUBLIC INTEREST LAW:
Where Law Meets Social Action

by ROBERT A. BAUM

1987
Oceana Publications, Inc.
London • Rome • New York

This is the eighty-sixth number in a series of LEGAL ALMANACS which bring you the law on various subjects in nontechnical language. These books do not take the place of your attorney's advice, but they can introduce you to your legal rights and responsibilities.

Library of Congress Cataloging-in-Publication Data

Baum, Robert A.
  Public interest law.

  (Legal almanac series ; no. 86)
  Includes index.
  1. Public interest law—United States.   I. Title.
II. Series.
KF390.5.P78B38   1986   349.73   86-28551
ISBN 0-379-11162-4   347.3

Manufactured in the United States of America

TABLE OF CONTENTS

INTRODUCTION

What is Public Interest Law?

"Public Interest Law" is the area where social conscience meets the law. Public interest lawyers seek to "advance the right of persons [or causes] who are victims of unnecessary and harmful abuses." Perhaps the most accepted definition of public interest law is that it is:

> The name given to efforts to provide legal representation to interests that historically have been unrepresented and under-represented in the legal process. These include not only the poor and disadvantaged, but ordinary citizens who, because they cannot afford lawyers to represent them, have lacked access to courtrooms, administrative agencies, and other legal forums in which basic policy decisions affecting their interests are made.

Council for Public Interest Law, *Balancing the Scales of Justice,* at 3 (1976) (hereinafter "Balancing the Scales,)

The American Bar Association's definition of public interest law is much broader and reflects its efforts to get lawyers involved in the *pro bono* process generally: "legal service provided without fee or at a substantially reduced fee, which falls into one or more of the following areas: (1) Poverty law . . .; (2) Civil Rights law . . .; (3) Public Rights law . . .; (4) Charitable Organization Representation . . .; and (5) Administration of Justice. . . ."

While the practice of public interest lawyers varies, one theme prevails: they "represent movements of people who throughout the history of this country have struggled

1

to protect and advance the elementary rights and interests against attempts by the government or big business to undermine or derail them." A. Kinoy, *Rights on Trial* at 2 (1980).

Oftentimes, public interest law issues affect large segments of society and the issues involved go beyond the interests of the immediate parties to a dispute, thus affecting the general public, e.g. seeking a declaration from the courts that the United States' participation in the Vietnam War, the Gramm-Rudman Act (which mandated a balanced budget for the federal government) or racial segregation, are unconstitutional. The impact of public interest law has been profound, as Supreme Court Justice Thurgood Marshall wrote:

> Public interest law seeks to fill some of the gaps in our legal system. Today's public interest lawyers have built upon the earlier successes of civil rights, civil liberties, and legal aid lawyers, but have moved into new areas. Before courts, administrative agencies and legislatures, they provide representation for a broad range of relatively powerless minorities—for example, to the mentally ill, to children, to the poor of all races. They also represent neglected interests that are widely shared by most of us as consumers, as workers, and as individuals in need of privacy and a healthy environment. These lawyers have, I believe, made an important contribution. They do not (nor should they) always prevail, but they have won many important victories for their clients. More fundamentally, perhaps, they have made our legal process work better. They have broadened the flow of information to decision makers. They have made it possible for administrators, legislators and judges to assess the

impact of their decisions in terms of all affected interests. And, by helping to open the doors to our legal system, they have moved us a little closer to the ideal of equal justice for all.

Ford Foundation and ABA Special Committee on Public Interest Practice, *Public Interest Law: Five Years Later,* at Forward (1976)

As Justice Marshall wrote, public interest law has affected the lives of all citizens. It has created new bodies of law to protect the rights of all groups, and has reshaped how our government and corporations function. It has, in short, had a major impact on the substantive and procedural development of American law.

Yet, public interest law also deals with individual problems, which are a reflection of a societal ill. Legal Aid Society lawyers, for example, represent those who are too poor to afford a lawyer, but who without the assistance of an attorney would be denied effective access to the legal system. A Legal Aid Society lawyer's day to-day cases may not have a large impact on society as a whole. But the collective work of all Legal Aid attorneys has tremendous impact on society: it gives the downtrodden the ability to fight against much stronger and wealthier elements, and to survive. The impact of Legal Aid programs in poverty areas is so strong that they are credited with diffusing the tensions in the inner city and helping to prevent riots.

For a public interest lawyer, the key question when asked to handle a case is whether the right or issue is important enough to warrant a major financial and time commitment. The amount of money recoverable — for the plaintiff or the lawyer — is not a determinative, or even usually an important factor. Rather, the determining factor is "what are the policy issues that require my personal (or organizational) involvement?"

3

The vast majority of public interest lawyers do not claim to represent the entire public interest. Rather, they represent parties that decision makers have not fully heard, and seek to vindicate rights that decision makers have overlooked or illegitimately compromised. In some cases, as Justice Douglas pointed out in *Sierra Club v. Morton*, the public interest attorney's real client-in-interest is not even a person, but rather is an inanimate subject such as trees and wildlife. Public interest lawyers therefore, usually play David to more traditionally represented Goliaths, such as large, corporate interests that shape governmental policy.

The overall goal of public interest law is to provide the same type of continuous assistance that corporate counsel provide to their clients. Yet the closer public interest lawyers get to that goal, the more criticism they engender, partly because "public interest law has involved working for goals far more congruent with the philosophy of the political left than the political right." (Stover, "The Importance of Economic Supply in Determining the Size and Quality of the Public Interest Law Bar," 16 Law & Society Review at 455 (1982)).

Obviously, there is no accepted definition of public interest law. This book looks at two types of public interest law — those issues that involve matters which affect a large segment of society, and the type of law which principally affects individuals, often described as "poverty law." Corporate litigation, where one corporation is battling another, although it may have a large impact on society (e.g. antitrust litigation), is not considered to be public interest litigation for purposes of this book.

The Need for Public Interest Attorneys

Because of the complex system of laws which legislatures and administrative agencies (usually composed of lawyers) and the courts (always composed of lawyers) have adopted, legal rights generally inure only to those who have the necessary skills to pursue their rights — i.e. lawyers and those who can afford them. Unfortunately, the legal profession has historically under-represented citizen interests, while over-representing corporate interests. For example, in 1978, of the approximately 700 lawyers in Washington, D.C. who specialized in communication law, only 6 represented citizen interests. As former American Bar Association President, Leonard Janofsky, told the Bar Association House of Delegates, "today the average person — unless [his or her claim] is covered by insurance or processed on a contingent fee basis — simply cannot afford the cost of litigation." Approximately 150 organizations represent themselves to be public interest organizations, and fewer than .1% of all attorneys claim to be public interest attorneys. As an example of how out numbered lawyers are who represent the public interest, consider that in 1978 during litigation to force the oil companies to refund approximately 1.3 billion dollars in overcharges to consumers, the oil companies listed thirty separate attorneys as their attorneys of records and they reportedly involved over one hundred attorneys in the case. The public interest in the matter was represented by three attorneys. Nonetheless, the public interest lawyers generally prevailed.

Chapter 1

THE ROLE OF PUBLIC INTEREST LAWYERS

Lobbying

Lobbying for public interest causes is increasingly a major effort of public interest groups. Although public interest lawyers are most noted for their litigation in which they participate, litigation is actually the last resort for public interest lawyers.

Part of this new focus on public interest lobbying is attributable to the growing conservatism of the courts with their increasingly limited construction of constitutional and statutory rights. President Reagan will have appointed approximately 50% of the federal judiciary before he leaves office in 1989; all federal judges are appointed for life. Also, public interest groups feel more comfortable lobbying now than they did in the past based on a decade or more of experience for the many public interest groups which were organized in the 1960s and 70s.

Lobbying of Administrative Agencies

A significant amount of public interest lobbying occurs at the administrative agency level. Agencies are charged with enacting regulations to carry out the laws which Congress has passed. Congress passes legislation which sets the general regulatory framework, but it is left to the agencies to enact regulations to enforce the congressional intent. The regulatory process is an ongoing one, with existing laws constantly being enforced through new regulations. Public interest groups therefore must closely monitor the activities of administrative agencies, and participate in guideline or rulemaking proceedings of the agencies. Furthermore, to successfully challenge an agency's regulations (under the Administrative Procedure Act (APA) 5 U.S.C. section 551 *et seq.),* a public interest group usually has to build a record during the agency proceedings to support its position. If they lose at the administrative level then they can go to court and attempt to prove that the agency's action was "arbitrary and capricious," e.g. not supported by the information on the hearing record.

At agency proceedings, public interest groups try to bring new ideas or information to the agency's attention, and assist in analyzing the scientific data and interpreting technical aspects of the law. However, an equally important role they serve is to provide opposition to industry pressures. As former EPA Administrator Douglas Costell stated: "we need the counter-pressure that public interest groups provide against business lobbies," which helps the agency to take a middle ground.

Participation of public interest groups in administrative hearings has had an "astonishingly effective impact," but is rarely the end in itself. If the public interest organization succeeds in getting a favorable regulation on one issue, their wealthier opposition is usually prepared to outspend and outmaneuver them on the numerous other issues before the agency. Furthermore, the wealthier groups who oppose the regulations are more likely to have access to the White House. Of particular concern is those groups' access to the Office of Management and Budget which operates without public input, but which by Executive Order 12291 has the authority to review all proposed agency rules and to require a cost benefit analysis before the rules are promulgated. The Office of Management and Budget has used the order to kill many health, safety, environmental and other rules without public input, although Congress has attempted to force them to make their decisionmaking process public.

Congressional Lobbying

Even if the public interest groups succeed administratively, powerful special interest groups may successfully lobby Congress to overturn the agency's decision. For example, for six years the Federal Trade Commission investigated unfair and deceptive practices in the used car business. In 1981 they proposed regulations which would require used car dealers to disclose known defects to purchasers of used cars. The FTC concluded that "many dealers do misrepresent or fail to disclose material factors relating to . . . the mechanical condition of vehicles offered for sale" and passed the disclosure regulations. After the dealers lost on the administrative level, they took their case, and money, to Congress. Because of earlier business pressure, Congress had established a "congressional veto" for FTC rules. Recognizing the potential to use the legislative veto, the used car dealers, through their trade associations, particularly the National Automobile Dealers Association (NADA), mobilized. With member car dealers in every congressional district, they personally lobbied their congressmen. But perhaps more importantly, 85 percent of the 206 co-sponsors of the used car veto resolution in the House received a total of $476,826 in campaign contributions from NADA. In other words, congressmen who received NADA money were over 3 times as likely to co-sponsor the veto resolution as those who did not get NADA money. In the Senate, the correlation between money and co-sponsorship was weaker, but still, a senator who received NADA money was approximately 33% more likely to have co-sponsored the veto resolution than those who did not.

Although the Supreme Court has declared the legislative veto to be unconstitutional, Congress can still restrict agency rulemaking by writing limitations into legislation. For example, in the Federal Trade Commission Appropriation Bill for 1982, the FTC was severely restricted from rulemaking in the areas of funeral homes and advertising to children. Furthermore, from 1982 to 1986 the FTC was not even able to get Congress to pass a funding reauthorization bill.

Public Interest Lobbying in Action

Perhaps the best example of a public interest lobbying effort which effectively used the skills of public interest lobbyists is the struggle for national parks in Alaska.

The idea of establishing national parks in Alaska went back to the 1920s. With the increase of development in Alaska in the late 1960s, the concept of national parks increased.

To cope with the anticipated future battle for the use of the Alaskan wilderness, in 1971 the Sierra Club established the "Alaska Coalition" for the primary purpose of lobbying for environmentally sound land set aside for national parks and wilderness areas. From 1971 to 1976 the "Alaska Coalition" was basically the Sierra Club, and its primary activity was to organize and analyze studies which volunteers and field representatives conducted about Alaska.

From their research, they devised a comprehensive plan for which areas should be set aside for wilderness and parks. In 1975, the first Alaska Wilderness Bill was introduced in Congress. Without sufficient organizational lobbying, this bill failed.

In 1976, the anti-environment chairman of the House Interior and Insular Affairs Committee, (which had primary jurisdiction over Alaskan wilderness issues) was defeated for reelection. The next most senior member of the interior committee, Bizz Johnson, was at least as anti-environmental as his predecessor. Environmental groups lobbied within the Democratic Party to stir up opposition to Johnson and support for Congressman Morris Udall, the second most senior member of the Committee and an environmental champion. At the same time, the environmentalists saw to it that Johnson was given the opportunity to chair another committee in the House. Given certainty of a fight for the chairmanship of the Interior Committee, and possible defeat or an uncontested chairmanship of another committee, Johnson abandoned his quest for the Interior Committee Chairmanship and left the position to Udall. The environmentalists scored their first major victory in the long struggle for a pro-environmental Alaska Wilderness Bill.

The second victory was easier. To ensure that the measure was given a favorable hearing, environmentalists prevailed on Chairman Udall to create a special general oversight subcommittee on Alaska, which would be responsible for the bill. Udall also agreed to appoint the environmentalist candidate, Congressman John Seiberling, to chair that committee.

From the coalition of environmental groups that banded together to assist Udall in his quest for the Interior Committee chairmanship, came the real "Alaska Coalition." Fifty environmental groups formed the New Alaska Coalition and each contributed a few staff or volunteers to assist the Coalition's efforts. Realizing that the Coalition might have a long existence, the Coalition incorporated and formed the Alaska Coalition, Inc. in 1978.

While the Coalition was organizing internally, it was mobilizing in the field, and conceived of a plan to have Congressman Seiberling's subcommittee hold hearings throughout the country. Seiberling agreed. This permitted the Coalition to organize and motivate its members to participate locally, where they received local press coverage that they otherwise would not have enjoyed.

The field hearings and environmentalists' studies created an enormous record which the Coalition needed to defend its bill (HR-39) against an array of opposition. The Coalition, which had a maximum staff of eighty people and budget of less than $300,000, had to contend with opposition which included Fortune 500 corporations such as Exxon, Atlantic Richfield Petroleum (ARCO), timber and mining interests, Congress' most powerful lobbying organization (National Rifle Association), and the lobby for Alaska business interests, which called itself "Citizens for Management of Alaskan Lands." One minor interest alone (US Borax), reportedly spent several million dollars to defeat the bill.

The Coalition never believed it could out-spend its opposition, but believed it could out-organize them. The Coalition sought out disparate groups to support its efforts, and gathered senior citizen, civic, labor, environmental and sportsmen groups, with a combined membership of over ten million people, to support the bill. These groups rallied their members to lobby Congressmen and Senators to support the bill and the Coalition mailed over one million pieces of literature to activist members. In addition, the Coalition's grassroots organizers were on the telephone throughout the country day and night, keeping the field organizers informed of the latest strategies, goals and facts. The field organizers passed that information on to active members in the community, who encouraged grassrooots letter writing, telephoning and personal visits to Congressmen and Senators, and further coalition building at the grassroots level.

Throughout 1979 and 1980, the Coalition and its opponents fought fierce battles during the numerous committee hearings, and lobbied intensely during the committee, floor and conference consideration of the bill. After the 1980 elections, the Coalition decided to compromise, and in December 1980, in a lame duck session, nine years of work ended when the Coalition asked its supporters in the House to accept the less than ideal Senate bill in its entirety, rather than continuing the fight.

Public Interest Lobbying in the '80s

Despite the enormous imbalance in funds, on the whole public interest lawyers have made their mark in Congress, the legislatures and administrative agencies. What they lack in financial resources, they attempt to make up for through mobilizing their constituencies and by working harder.

The Alaska Coalition battle has had a lasting impact on public interest lobbying. Numerous citizen groups learned from the Coalition's experience, and have established permanent field offices to organize grassroots support on legislative matters. Furthermore, they have learned how to organize internally to best be able to organize their membership. As Ralph Nader explained about his lobbying organization, Congress Watch:

> Since Congress Watch is not equipped with the lavish resources of our corporate counterparts, we depend on our skill and savvy in analyzing legislation, providing incisive testimony to congressional committees working with citizen coalitions and conducting aggressive media relations. In addition, the Congress Watch Field Office provides vital grassroots lobbying support on selected legislative issues.

For a public interest group to win a major legislative victory requires skilled leadership, tenacity, flexibility, and patience. In practice, all positions within the organization are inextricably intertwined. A successful lobbying effort requires that the leadership be available for personal lobbying and to join the field organizers in the field to rally public support. Researchers provide the arguments for the group's position, which the media experts and fundraisers skillfully use. The fundraisers use the heightened public awareness to raise funds for specific campaigns, and the lobbyists use the combined resources—leadership, research, money, heightened public awareness and activism—to influence legislators. This self-perpetuating cycle distinguishes public interest lobbying from other lobbying efforts. While traditional (e.g., corporate) lobbying often times relies on a campaign by well-paid lobbyists with little constituent involvement, public interest lobbying relies on constituent involvement, aided by professional, low-paid, but zealous lobbyists. As former FTC chairman Michael Pertschuk observed: "Public interest lobbyists' raw material is the unfocused energy of the public will. To succeed, the lobbyist must focus and unleash the energy that will move legislative mountains."

With so much "energy," or at least attempts to garner such energy from its members, lobbyists are faced with the challenge of focusing the activists so that they do not inadvertently steer the campaign off course, while keeping them motivated for a long campaign. As Common Cause founder John Garner noted, "in Common Cause, we guard against dissipation of energy by simple philosophy: With rare exceptions, we do nothing but fight specific battles — legal or legislative. We enter each battle seeking a specific outcome. We stay until we win or lose."

Public interest organizing continues to become more organized. In the fall of 1984, former Common Cause Chairman David Cohen and former FTC chairman Michael Pertschuk founded "Public Advocates" in Washington, D.C. to help public interest groups (which they define as civil and human rights, public health, arms control, environment, consumer, tax, justice and economic opportunity groups that lacked the political resources) intervene in politics to redress the balance of power to the benefit of the public. Public Advocates seeks to help "citizen groups" to "match their adversaries' professionalism and overcome money, privilege and technical advantages of special interest lobbies." While the public interest community recognizes that it will never have the funds to match their adversaries, they hope through the efforts of trained, volunteer lobbyists, to be able to match their clout.

To effectuate this goal, Public Advocates perform three functions: counselling non-profit groups concerning their needs, strategies and tactics, and how to attract media attention; teaching lobbying and media skills; and clinical training. Once volunteer lobbyists are trained, they are matched with a public interest group and represent those public interest groups in need of citizen voices against professional lobbyists.

One of Public Advocates most successful campaigns was on behalf of the Children's Defense Fund. For eight years, the Children's Defense Fund had been urging Congress to broaden the scope of the Medicaid Program to include married mothers and their children. In 1985, they asked the Public Advocates for help. Public Advocates matched the Children's Defense Fund with 16 trained volunteer lobbyists, who donated approximately $100,000 worth of service to the campaign. According to the Children's Defense Fund, these volunteer lobbyists made the "crucial difference" in their long awaited victory.

The Continuing Need for Public Interest Litigation

Despite a focus on lobbying, public interest law will always depend on litigation to be effective. For example, even when a public interest organization succeeds legislatively, they face enormous difficulties in getting the administrative agencies to implement their legislative mandate. For example, in 1972 Congress passed amendments to the Federal Water Pollution Control Act that set the goal of restoring all of the nation's water supply to a "fishable and swimmable" condition by 1983, and completely ending water pollution by 1985. Congress gave the Environmental Protection Agency (EPA) responsibility for ensuring that the Act's goals were met. EPA was to set standards and regulations and then enforce them.

To ensure enforcement of the Clean Water Act, the Natural Resources Defense Council set up a project to oversee the EPA's applications of the law. For this purpose, they hired scientists, engineers, and lawyers. They actively participated in the EPA's rulemaking proceedings. EPA missed the rulemaking deadlines almost immediately. After EPA missed 14 rulemaking deadlines within the first few months of the Act, NRDC brought a lawsuit that resulted in a court ordered schedule for publishing these regulations. *NRDC v. Fry,* 5 Environmental Law Reporter, 20173 (D.D.C. 1974). The NRDC then went back to the agency to participate in the rulemaking process.

The need to resort to litigation is particularly acute when Congress gives the executive branch discretionary authority, reviewable by the Courts. In some such circumstances, Congress may have legislated as specifically as possible and further Congressional lobbying would not be effective. For example, the Voting Rights Act of 1965 (as amended in 1982) requires southern states and others to submit any changes in election procedures to the U.S. Justice Department for clearance. The Justice Department is supposed to ensure that the proposed changes do not result in discrimination, even if the result was not intended. Yet the Justice Department has not only routinely approved such changes without investigating their impact, but they have argued in court for a restrictive interpretation of their duties under the Voting Rights Act. Without the executive branch to enforce the laws, public interest groups have no choice but to act as "private attorneys general." Without litigation, "many a well drawn law has remained mere words in a statute book because of ineffective enforcement." Public interest law firms have therefore become a primary force behind enforcing those laws.

Litigation is also necessary to preserve basic constitutional rights which legislators would not address (e.g., to prevent school districts from removing books from school library shelves, because fundamentalists thought the books were obscene). As many groups have realized, particularly in the days of a more liberal judiciary, "the law is the great equalizer. All it takes is one person with a good legal argument that can convince one judge, and that's it."

Litigation

Congress has enacted substantial amounts of legislation to cure social problems, such as discrimination, environmental degradation and abuse of the poor. At an increasing rate, the federal administrative agencies have not enforced the rights and protections which such laws afford, and public interest groups have had to seek judicial enforcement. It is fair to say that public interest disputes are resolved more often by the courts than by Congress.

> Disadvantaged groups are highly dependent upon the judicial process as a means of pursuing their policy interests, usually because they are temporarily or even permanently, disadvantaged in terms of their abilities to attain successfully their goals in the electoral process, within the elected political institutions, or in the bureaucracy. If they are to succeed at all in the pursuit of their goals, they are almost compelled to resort to litigation.

Note, "Public Interest Law", 35 Mercer L. Rev. 864 (1984)

That is, even when non-litigation avenues are available, litigation is often the most desirable course, particularly when the political climate is contrary to the public interest groups' position.

> Under the conditions of modern government, litigation may well be the sole practicable avenue open to minorities to petition for redress of grievances. . . .For such a group, association for litigation may well be the most effective form of political association.

NAACP v. Button, 371 U.S. 415, 429, 431 (1963)

Through litigation, public interest lawyers have affectuated reforms in all aspects of life, including in the essential areas of housing, work place safety, equal employment opportunity, minority and civil rights and in the clean environment.

History of Public Interest Law for Individual Clients
"Poverty Law"

The origins of Public Interest Law can be traced to the Magna Carta of 1215 A.D. in which King John pledged, "to no one will we sell, to no one will we refuse or delay, right, or justice," and to the 1495 statute of Henry VII, which guaranteed free, assigned counsel for indigents: ". . .the justices. . .shall assign the same poor person or persons counsel learned, by their discretions which shall give counsel, nothing taking for the same;. . . in likewise the justices shall appoint attorney and attorneys for the same poor person or persons. . ." Statute of Henry VII, 1495, ii NHEN. 7, C.12 quoted in E. Johnson, Jr., *Justice and Reform* (1974) at 3. Those principles were not imported to the colonies, where the Constitution guaranteed due process of law, but did not provide for mandatory *pro-bono* assistance of counsel.

The first reported legal aid type of organization was not formed until after the Civil War. In 1865 the Freedman's Bureau established a program to provide legal aid to Blacks in civil and criminal cases through use of legal counsel which the organization hired for the client. This first concerted effort to provide legal services to indigents ended only three years later. In 1876, the German Society of New York tried a different approach to provide legal services to exploited German immigrants, by hiring staff attorneys. That society eventually became the New York Legal Aid Society, which continues to provide legal services to indigents.

In Chicago in 1886 the second legal aid organization, The Protective Agency for Women and Children, was established to fight "the great number of seductions and debaucheries of young girls under the guise of proferred employment" and in 1888 the Chicago Ethical Culture

Society established the Bureau of Justice. That Bureau was the first legal aid society opened to all people, regardless of nationality or gender. Thereafter, the legal aid movement grew rapidly for a short period, to six cities by 1900, 28 by 1914, and 41 by 1917. That year legal aid organizations employed 62 full-time attorneys and 113 part-time attorneys and handled 117,201 cases.

Despite the increasing interest in the availability of legal services for indigents, the legal aid movement essentially stagnated by 1918 with court fees, litigation expenses and lawyers fees keeping the courthouse doors closed to many. Then, a twenty-nine year old attorney, Reginald Heber Smith, set out to change the entire legal aid process. In his book, *Justice and the Poor* (1919) at 11-12, he wrote:

> The essentially conservative bench and bar will vehemently deny any suggestion that there is no law for the poor, but as legal aid societies know, such is the belief today of a multitude of humble, entirely honest people, in the light of their experience which appears as a simple truth. . . Differences in the ability of classes to use the machinery of the law, if permitted to remain, lead inevitably to disparity between the rights of classes... And when the law recognizes and enforces a distinction between classes, revolution ensues or democracy is at an end.

For the first time, the organized bar in America was directly confronted with the notion that it had a responsibility to assist those who could not afford to pay for meaningful access to the courts. Smith's solution to that problem was to organize a national association of legal aid offices. Smith stated that a central legal aid organization was necessary because:

20

For the future, the work is too great to be conducted in slip-shod way, and its extension into new fields is too important to be left to a hit or miss policy. . . Matters of policy should become uniform as rapidly as possible. . . Some initiative must be manifested in establishing societies where they are needed. There must be some central body authorized to represent and speak for the organized legal aid movement in the councils of the Bar, at the meetings of charities and in the law school conference. . . If their voice is to be heard, as it has not been in the past, and if their opinions are to carry weight, they must present a united front, having clearly formulated their aims and speak with singleness of mind to a definite. . . purpose.

Justice and the Poor at 245-6.

To further the cause, Smith sought financial and organizational aid from the American Bar Association. In 1923, Smith's efforts sowed substantial progress, with the formation of the National Association of Legal Aid Organizations (now the National Legal Aid and Defenders Association, "NLADA"). Shortly thereafter, several states and local bar associations formed committees to promote legal assistance to poor people in their areas. Smith's efforts between 1920 and 1930 produced thirty new legal aid organizations, and financial resources available for those organizations more than doubled. Furthermore, Smith promoted the idea that lawyers had a greater obligation to society than handling individual cases: they must also work legislatively and at the appellate level to create basic changes in society's treatment of the poor. Although Smith initiated the idea of public interest impact litigation, little such work was done during his time.

The Legal Aid movement followed an inconsistent path in later years. During the depression, the case loads of its offices throughout the country swelled. But because the private bar, which funded the movement, was also hurt by the depression, contributions to legal aid societies decreased. For example, in 1934 only 229 of New York City's 17,000 practicing attorneys contributed to Legal Aid. Legal Aid programs became so overwhelmed with the bulging case loads and lack of resources that the system became practically paralyzed. As a result, after 1934 citizens apparently assumed that resort to Legal Aid Societies was useless, and the Societies' case load decreased.

The Legal Aid movement remained essentially static until 1950, when Great Britain instituted a government financed legal services program. The threat that the United States government might take a similarly active role in providing legal services, thereby endangering the lawyers' unbridled ability to control the legal system, caused American lawyers to act. Money began to flow into the NLADA coffers, so that within the decade from 1949 to 1959, the percentage of larger cities without legal aid offices was reduced from 43% to 21% and the number of legal aid and defender offices almost tripled.

As the country went through the early 1960s, it became apparent that the private bar would not adequately fund Legal Aid. Whereas in the nation as a whole there was one lawyer available to serve every 560 people, there was only one lawyer available per 120,000 indigent persons (the equivalent of 400 full-time lawyers were available to serve almost 50 million Americans). In 1964, there were only 250 staffed civil Legal Aid offices in the country. Nine cities with populations of over 1 million people, 15 slightly smaller communities and 105 communities with over 100,000 people had no Legal Aid office. Where there were offices, many Legal Aid attorneys carried case loads of over 1,000 cases, which almost guaranteed that no client's case would receive much attention. As one study noted:

> Three out of four accepted applicants for legal aid receive only a single brief consultation; only a minimal amount of time is given to the investigation of fact, to legal research and drafting of legal documents, and to court work. Many offices, in fact, are incapable of handling cases that require extensive investigation or time consuming litigation. The situation is further aggravated by low salaries, high turnover in personnel and inadequate direction by "disinterested or inactive boards of directors." There is little time or incentive to enter into a contest over legal principle, to make or alter a law, or to combat institutionalized sources of injustice.

Carlin, Howard, and Messinger, *Civil Justice and the Poor* at 50 (1966).

The voluntary redistribution of the nation's legal resources was not succeeding: less than .2% of the nation's annual expenditures for legal resources were devoted to serving the 25% of the population who could not afford to hire an attorney. Furthermore, even where money was provided to legal aid organizations, it oftentimes was provided with limitations (real or perceived) on how it could be used, so that claims against local merchants and landlords would not be pursued and clients would not be assisted in filing for bankruptcy since that action would make it more difficult for the contributors to collect debts from legal aid clients.

The breakthrough began in 1965, when as part of the war on poverty, President Johnson established the Office of Economic Opportunity (OEO) and in 1966 when Congress specifically authorized OEO to provide funds for legal services to the poor. The result was dramatic. In 1965, the last year before federal funding, the budgets of all legal aid societies totaled $5,375,890, and they employed the equivalent of 400 full-time attorneys. By 1968, the OEO legal services budget was $40,000,000, and 2,400 full-time attorneys were employed.

With the infusion of federal funds, legal aid offices began to pursue cases they previously avoided. While legal aid lawyers did not litigate any case before the United States Supreme Court until 1965, from 1965 to 1972 they filed over 200 cases with the high court. (Of the 136 Supreme Courts cases which were decided on the merits, the Legal Aid position prevailed in 73.) By one estimate, between 1967 and 1968, legal aid societies increased their law reform (impact litigation) activities by over 500%.

The invigoration of legal services for the poor did not go well in many areas of the country, however. Governors of California, Florida, Connecticut, Arizona and Missouri vetoed the legal services budgets, as the statute permitted them to do. Senator George Murphy attempted to limit legal services attorneys to represent only defendants (i.e. prohibiting them from filing lawsuits) stating:

> Legal services attorneys are not only working as defense counsel, they will also bring a cause of action as well as defend an indigent in a suit. They will do one thing more. They will institute test cases. Recently, in this manner, they have begun to challenge our laws too often. . . .there are too many cases for legal services to handle without involving themselves in these test cases.

113 Congressional Record part 21 at 27871,27872 (Oct. 4, 1967).

Large impact litigation cases which infuriated Senator Murphy and others included successful lawsuits to stop the importation of foreign workers to farms in the Southwest, (thereby reducing the supply of such cheap labor and improving the bargaining position of low paid farm workers); to strike down substitute parent and residency requirements to be eligible for welfare assistance; and to require equal spending in school districts, to force a redistribution of state expenditures to benefit children in poor communities. Successful lawsuits such as those affected the finances of all levels of governments and large corporations.

By 1974, the Nixon administration had enough of the government paying attorneys to sue it, and they moved to abolish the legal services program. Partisan fighting was so fierce that the entire OEO budget was frozen. Under pressure from the American Bar Association, Legal Aid clients and staff, and other lawyers, Congress that year voted to form an independent Legal Services Corporation (LSC) with a $70 million budget. Ironically, Nixon's last act as President before resigning was to sign the Legal Service Corporation Act.

Most of the new Legal Services Corporation money went to existing Legal Aid Programs, which already had a staff of approximately 2,000 attorneys. However, restrictions were placed on LSC attorneys to prevent their programs from engaging in political activities, such as lobbying, and to curtail use of class action lawsuits. In almost every year since, attempts have been made to limit the independence of Legal Aid attorneys. For example, in 1977 Congress voted to prohibit legal aid attorneys from handling school desegregation cases or representing illegal aliens, selective service cases, or abortion cases.

Legal Services Corporation funds, through grants, independent private corporations which hire attorneys to provide legal assistance to individuals, and to provide centers for legal information and backup support to the grantees. [See appendix II] The grantees also oftentimes provide the services of social workers, community workers, and/or legal assistants who were from the area and are able to help the client personally and will work in the community on such projects as education and preventive law projects.

By 1981, several important goals of the legal services program had been met; one clinic was funded in every county in the United States, and two attorneys were available for every 10,000 eligible clients. Despite these gains only 20% of the legal needs of the poor people were being served by the program.

Nonetheless, in 1981, the Reagan administration asked Congress to abolish the Legal Services Corporation. The Reagan administration philosophy was that the private bar should be responsible for providing legal services to the poor, without federal government assistance. Congress recognized that two centuries of history showed that the private bar would not adequately provide services to the poor in this country, and they refused to abolish the program. As a compromise, the Legal Services Corporation budget was slashed 25% in one year, from $321 million to $241 million. This caused massive layoffs (including loss of approximately 25% of the full time legal aid attorneys, from 6,599 in 1980 to 4,766 in 1983), closing of Legal Services offices, and clients with active cases without lawyers. Also, further restrictions were put on the ability of Legal Services lawyers to represent their clients, particularly in impact and class action lawsuits. Those changes were designed to tie the Legal Services grantees to litigating cases which would not alter the existing economic system. While technically the attorneys still have jurisdiction over the bread and butter issues

such as divorce, domestic cases, assistance from government aid programs such as Aid to Families with Dependent Children, food stamps, Medicare, Social Security and Disability payments, landlord/tenant, creditor matters and public housing disputes, in reality most Legal Aid offices have been forced to establish broad classes of cases which they cannot accept, regardless of the impact on the individual or community, because of manpower shortages.

Congress also ordered the LSC to require grantees to allocate 10% of their budget to pay private attorneys (this was raised to 12.5% in 1983) to represent legal aid eligible clients. The argument for distribution of legal services funds to private attorneys is: (1) it gives legal aid clients greater freedom of choice in selecting an attorney; (2) the use of private attorneys minimizes any stigma to poor people who need legal services (e.g. they do not have to go to "separate but equal" law offices); (3) the more lawyers involved in poverty law, the more successful it will become, (the poor will benefit from the experience of the entire Bar, and the entire Bar will be sensitized to the problems of the poor); (4) private attorneys have more freedom from political interference and are better able to maintain a proper attorney/client relationship (i.e. such attorneys will decide how to handle cases based on the merits, not on their private agendas for what social policy should be); (5) the program makes more sense in rural areas where clients are widely dispersed; (6) there is less chance for social activism by spreading the work around; and (7) such a program fulfills the Legal Aid goal of equal access to justice.

However, that program has created resentment in the Legal Aid bar because, while trained Legal Aid attorneys were laid off, inexperienced private attorneys were hired in their place, and other Legal Aid attorneys had to divert

their attention from productive cases to train these inexperienced private attorneys. Therefore, some attorneys argue that private bar involvement is not cost effective, particularly to train a general litigator to handle one or two "poverty law" cases such as welfare denials. They further argue that it is illogical to pay private attorneys at a much higher rate than LSC staff attorneys are paid, since legal aid attorneys and private bar attorneys recover the same amount an hour when attorneys fees are recovered, but fees collected for staff attorney work yields much more back into the Legal Aid system. There is also some fear that the private bar attorneys are the less successful attorneys, and they take Legal Aid cases because they need the money and/or experience, and they will not give Legal Aid clients the same treatment as other paying clients receive.

Legal aid attorneys also argue that the private bar requirement insures that legal problems of the poor will be litigated on a fragmented basis. Full-time legal services attorneys are more likely to see day-to-day problems as a pattern, to know their community's needs, and more likely to deal with the problem in a concerted manner on broad based terms with which they are familiar. Furthermore, by maintaining control over all cases, the Legal Aid attorneys are better able to allocate their resources by prioritizing them in a way that will be most cost effective, and to combine cases into class action lawsuits. Attorneys who are only assigned one or two cases in an area may not have the knowledge, funds or dedication to pursue class wide relief.

In addition to splintering the delivery of Legal Aid, the LSC was placed in a state of chaos with the presidential appointment of a Board of Directors who had previously urged the abolition of the Legal Services Corporation. The Board attempted to defund certain legal aid programs,

conducted surprise raids on legal services grantees to search files, substantially increased payments and expenses to themselves, and ordered stricter reporting procedures for grantees, while reducing the grantees' budgets. In short, the dream of Reginald Smith, that legal services should be available to all who need it, is considered to be in greater danger now than in several decades. Yet, because of these dangers, the private bar has stepped in with private bar involvement projects.

Role of Private Lawyers' Organizations in Public Interest Law

The American Bar Association

In 1975, the American Bar Association House of Delegates resolved that "the basic responsibility of each lawyer engaged in the practice of law [is] to provide legal services without fee or at substantially reduced fee in areas of poverty, civil rights law, charitable organizations and administration of justice." In that year, the average nonbillable number of hours devoted to public interest work was 27 hours per lawyer per year. The ABA has not conducted a follow-up survey on private attorney *pro bono* work by hours, but it estimates that 10.6% of the attorneys participate in uncompensated *pro bono* programs. Estimated participation ranges from 2.6% of practicing attorneys in the District of Columbia to 54.6% in New Hampshire.

The ABA has established a *"pro bono* recruitment project"* whose purpose is to "fill the gaps caused by federal cutbacks [in legal aid] as well as to fulfill the profession's responsibility to the public." [See appendix III for a list of those projects] To achieve this goal, the ABA has granted funds on a one year, non-renewable basis, of up to $20,000, to help local Bar Associations to

establish *pro bono* projects. The ABA's goal for the local *pro bono* projects is initially to attract 100 law firms, which have not previously been involved in *pro bono* activity, to accept one *pro bono* case. These firms are recruited to handle individual problems, such as domestic relations and landlord/tenant disputes. Beyond encouragement, the ABA *pro bono* recruitment committees are to act as resource centers for the volunteer attorneys, to provide those attorneys with information about local training programs and support services such as library facilities and "brief banks." The ABA committee will also loan the volunteer law firms up to $3,000 for a case. The amount of the loan increases with the seriousness of the case, the number of people affected, and the possibility of the case setting legal precedent. If the attorney does not recover any legal fees, or his client does not obtain any recovery or return of costs, then the law firm is not obligated to repay the loan.

The ABA has been criticized for the relatively insignificant role it has played in even low impact *pro bono* work, not to mention class action impact litigation. Between 1981 and 1985, it granted a total of $615,000 in one-year non-renewable grants to establish *pro bono* programs, which is a small percentage of the ABA's annual budget for even one year. More significantly, the ABA after years of debate has refused to adopt mandatory *pro bono* activity as part of its rules of professional conduct. Rather, the rule it has adopted, Rule of Professional Conduct 6.1, states:

> A lawyer should render public interest legal service. A lawyer may discharge this responsibility by providing professional services at no fee or a reduced fee to persons of limited means or to public service or charitable groups or organizations, by service and activities for improving the

law, the legal system, or the legal profession, and by financial support for organizations that provide legal services to persons of limited means.

The official comments to the Rule state: "this rule . . . is not intended to be enforced through disciplinary process." The ABA encourages each attorney to dedicate forty hours per year to public interest work, but does not enforce that recommendation.

In addition to not requiring attorneys to participate in *pro bono* activities, the ABA itself rarely becomes involved in important public interest litigation. For example, the ABA Board of Governors refused to permit various committees of the ABA to file an *amicus* brief in *Jean v. Nelson*, to assert that excludable aliens have Fifth Amendment rights, or in *Evans v. Jeff D.*, to state that it is unethical for government attorneys to insist that public interest attorneys waive their right to attorney fees in exchange for settlement of public interest cases. The last civil rights *amicus* brief the ABA filed was in 1982, for a stay of execution in a death penalty case. In the 1980's, they filed a total of four *amicus* briefs with the high court, and they have not directly participated in any public interest cases.

The ABA however has had an important impact in organizing the private bar to replace the legal services lost through the LSC cutbacks. In 1980, fewer than 50 bar associations had private bar involvement projects. By the spring of 1986, that number had risen to 533, of which almost two thirds of the attorneys worked *pro bono* (the others, of course, benefited from the 12.5% LSC private bar funding requirement). By one estimate, Legal Services is operating at about 80% of what it did before the Reagan Administration cutbacks, mostly because of private bar involvement. Furthermore, the ABA has encouraged state bar associations to establish programs for attorneys to place clients' money which is held in trust into interest bearing accounts, with the interest to go to legal services or *pro bono* programs.

Alternative Bar Associations

Numerous bar associations have been established in response to the ABA's perceived conservatism and historic minimal support for social causes. Many such bar associations address specific needs of their members (e.g. the Women's Bar Association, the National Bar Association (for Black attorneys), and the Mexican-American Bar Association).

The oldest and most diverse of such alternative bar associations is the National Lawyers Guild (NLG) which was founded in 1937 to provide a national alternative to the racially segregated and anti-New Deal position of the ABA. Upon its founding, the NLG began filing *amicus* briefs in support of "progressive" legislation such as the National Labor Relations Act and Social Security, which the ABA opposed. The Guild has remained on the left of the national legal community throughout its existence, but it has often been the forerunner for causes which the majority of attorneys later endorsed. While the ABA has often eschewed becoming involved in political contro-versies, the Guild has actively sought to be the conscience of the legal community. For its efforts, the Guild was branded "the legal arm of the communist party" in the 1950's and was slated to be placed on the Attorney General's list of subversive organizations. The Guild successfully fought the Attorney General's efforts in the courts, until the Attorney General withdrew its threatened listing. (Ironically, the Guild's most expensive and lengthy legal battle has been its lawsuit against the FBI for spying and wiretapping on Guild members and breaking into the various Guild offices to steal membership lists and other materials.)

The Guild has been the progressive bar's torchbearer, particularly in two areas: race relations and foreign policy. In the 1940's, while the ABA was still segregated, the Guild opposed discrimination, including fighting the poll tax, and led investigations into race riots. In the 1960's, the Guild became the first national organization to open an office in the south, with the goal of providing large scale legal assistance for blacks. For that purpose, they brought in lawyers from around the country, because southern lawyers were generally unwilling to represent blacks.

While the ABA has generally supported the incumbent administration's foreign policy, the NLG has often times opposed it. The Guild was the only national lawyers' organization to set up local committees to help draft eligible men to avoid the Vietnam era draft, particularly blacks, and established an office in the Philippines to help military personnel stationed there to avoid going to Vietnam. The Guild also brought lawsuits directly, and filed *amicus* briefs, in several cases which sought to have the Vietnam war declared unconstitutional. Currently, the ABA supports the administration's Central American policies, while the Guild has filed an *amicus* brief in the World Court to have United States' actions against Nicaragua declared illegal, and to require the United States to admit refugees from El Salvador and Guatemala as political refugees. The Guild is typical of public interest lawyer organizations, in that it relies almost exclusively on volunteer lawyers to perform its legal work.

Lawyers' Committee for Civil Rights Under Law

Soon after the Civil Rights Act of 1964 went into effect, seven middle-age black workers at a major paper mill in Natchez, Mississippi began looking for a lawyer to help them obtain the rights that act promised.

Though nearly half of the population of Natchez was black, only 200 of the mill's 1,200 employees were black, and they were restricted for the most part to the lowest paid jobs. The seven black men had repeatedly watched younger, less senior, white workers trained, apprenticed, and promoted, while they and other black workers were held in dead end positions.

The seven black men were unable to afford legal fees. On their own the workers sent letters of complaint to the Equal Employment Opportunity Commission [without results]. . . . . They struggled on, mostly unassisted, for ten years, with little impact on the discriminatory patterns at the mill. Then, taking a day off from work in 1976, all seven men drove the seventy miles from Natchez to Jackson to meet with staff attorneys at the Mississippi Office of the Lawyers' Committee for Civil Rights Under Law. . . [T]he Lawyers' Committee attorney filed a Title VII employment discrimination suit on the worker's behalf, charging the mill not only with discriminating in hiring and promotion, but also in using its testing and seniority programs to keep black workers in the least desirable jobs.

Lawyers for the mill initiated a series of procedural maneuvers that threatened to smother the case. The Lawyers' Committee attorney, and a young, black sole practitioner from Jackson who was assisting in the litigation, soon found themselves overwhelmed. Faced with the need to take several depositions concurrently, a court-imposed gag order, a refusal by the mill to answer any interrogatories and a 90 day discovery deadline that was fast running out, the workers' two attorneys felt, as one of them said, "like a row boat filling with water." It became clear that they could not continue to carry the case on their own. A massive infusion of help was essential. An emergency call was placed to the Lawyers' Committee's national headquarters in Washington, asking attorneys there to find a private law firm that could enter the case immediately.

Within an hour, the National Committee had reached Paul, Weiss, Rifkind, Wharton and Garrison in New York and explained the situation. By the next morning, the firm had an attorney working full time on the case.

A few days later, the Paul, Weiss attorney went to Natchez to meet with the seven black workers. He introduced himself, explained his plans for the case, and asked whether the men wanted him to represent them. One of the workers, speaking for them all, replied:

"We'd been trying for ten years to get a lawyer on this case. When I saw your firm's letterhead with all those names on it, I just sat down and cried."

He then added: "And I said to myself, 'praise the Lord, at last we've got as many as they do.'"

Lawyers Committee for Civil Rights Under Law *Fifteenth Anniversary Report* at 9 - 10 (1978).

The Lawyers' Committee for Civil Rights Under Law ("Lawyers' Committee" or "LCCRUL") was established in 1963 while the south was torn by racial violence. President John F. Kennedy and Attorney General Robert F. Kennedy sought to mobilize the resources of the American bar in the wake of outright disregard for civil rights in the south, including police violence, mass roundups and arrest, illegal detention, the passage and enforcement of the illegal ordinances to break up protests, and a pledge by Alabama Governor George C. Wallace to use National Guard troops to prevent a black from registering at the University of Alabama. President Kennedy called 250 of the nation's leading lawyers, including law school deans, local Bar leaders and former presidents of the American Bar Association, attorneys general, solicitors general, and assistant attorneys general to the White House on June 21, 1963 and appealed for their support to restore civil rights in the south. The appeal was particularly urgent because southern laws could not and would not protect the rights of civil rights workers there, and without an infusion of volunteer lawyers from around the nation, worse violence and lawlessness could be expected. From that White House meeting, LCCRUL was established.

In the summers of 1963 and 1964 LCCRUL began to meet the President's desires by sending volunteer lawyers to Mississippi. In 1965, it opened a full-time office in Jackson, Mississippi, to protect civil rights in the south on a year round basis. (LCCRUL closed its Jackson, Mississippi office in 1986, but maintains its headquarters in Washington, D.C. and has independent affiliates in Boston, Chicago, Denver, Los Angeles, Philadelphia and San Francisco.)

LCCRUL is unique because of its organization and resources. It is not a membership organization: it has only 163 members, all of whom serve on its Board of Trustees. Those Trustees are from the pinnacle of government, academia, and private law firms, and are able to muster the nation's best legal resources. In its 20 year history, LCCRUL estimates that it has infused over 30 million dollars in *pro bono* services of the private bar into civil rights work, and such donations are expanding (e.g. last year LCCRUL estimated that over 4.1 million dollars in legal services were donated to Lawyers' Committee cases.) As LCCRUL states, "the strength of the Lawyers' Committee Program lies in its access to contributed services of the private bar."

The importance of LCCRUL to the civil rights community cannot be over stated. The $30 million of donated labor it marshalled has been used almost exclusively for impact litigation, usually in crucial ways. For example, LCCRUL is credited with saving the NAACP from bankruptcy when angry southern white businessmen sued them and won a 1.25 million dollars judgment in a Mississippi court. After the NAACP lost at the trial level, they were given the choice of either paying the 1.25 million dollars judgment or posting a 1.5 million dollars supersedeas bond to forestall attachment of their assets while their appeal is pending. Either choice would have bankrupted the organization.

The Lawyers' Committee called a meeting at which the following ensued:

> At that meeting, it was agreed that the NAACP's best hope for winning emergency relief was to get into federal court as quickly as possible, for there was little chance that the Mississippi state courts would overturn the chancery court's decision. The Lawyers' Committee called the Washington, D.C. law firm of Hogan & Hartson and asked them to explore that approach. Within hours,

Hogan & Hartson had three lawyers working on the case. That team was expanded to five after a weekend of almost round-the clock research. In the meantime, lawyers from Wilmer, Cutler & Pickering were working on possible state relief.

Legal teams from both Wilmer, Cutler and Hogan & Hartson worked feverishly over the next few weeks preparing the papers for their appeals. When they needed affidavits or on the scene advice or background information, either the Mississippi Office of the Lawyers' Committee or the NAACP staff provided what was requested. Only this infusion of private firm resources, coupled with the specialized back-up work of the Committee's civil rights staff, enabled the lawyers to meet the filing deadlines that were just a month away.

On Friday morning, October 1, the Wilmer, Cutler team prepared to make its appeal to the Mississippi Supreme Court in Jackson and the Hogan & Hartson team was in Oxford ready to make its case to the federal district court. The federal court acted first, granting a ten day temporary restraining order relieving the NAACP from paying the bond only hours before payment was due.

LCCRUL, *Fifteenth Annual Report* at 19-20

Eventually, the United States Supreme Court ruled in favor of the NAACP, *NAACP v. Claiborne Hardware Co.,* 458 U.S. 886 (1982), but the organization might not have survived to enjoy its victory if LCCRUL had not existed to coordinate the relief effort.

Role of Private Law Firms

Corporate Law Firms

When corporate law firms put their resources behind a public interest case, they can achieve significant results. For example, in the landmark case of *Gideon v. Wainwright,* which established criminal defendants' rights to appointed counsel in cases where imprisonment was a possible punishment, litigation at the Supreme Court was prepared and argued on a *pro bono* basis by future Justice Abe Fortas, a member of the law firm of Arnold & Porter.

Although numerous law firms participate in *pro bono* projects, one of the most institutionalized *pro bono* programs in the country is that of Hogan & Hartson, which has a special department devoted to public interest law. That program was established in 1970 by Judge John Ferren as a way of centralizing public interest law within the firm and thereby maximizing its impact, and to attract top law school graduates who might otherwise reject corporate law firms in favor of a career in public interest law. At Hogan & Hartson, a partner heads the department for three to four years, is assisted by a senior associate who serves the department for one and a half years, and by two rotating associates who work in the department four months each. The partner, in addition to litigating his own *pro bono* cases, attempts to spread *pro bono* work to the other 210 lawyers at the firm. Hogan & Hartson represents or has represented many civil rights and environmental groups, usually in litigation against the federal or state governments. In addition they handle impact litigation of which they become aware but which lacks organizational backing.

Large law firms have two distinct advantages in public interest cases that smaller firms or organizations do not have: the ability to rapidly mobilize large numbers of attorneys to work on a case, and the ability to financially absorb the cost of protracted litigation. For example, in 1986 Hogan & Hartson represented the American Civil Liberties Union and People for the American Way as intervenors in a lawsuit which 600 Christian fundamentalists filed in an attempt to have many textbooks in Alabama declared unconstitutionally "infected with humanism," in violation of the First Amendment's mandate of separation of church and state. The firm devoted six or seven lawyers on a part and full time basis to the case, which would cost over one hundred thousand dollars in attorney's fees, if the clients were to be billed. Such requirement of resources was so substantial that Alabama's second largest law firm was unable to take the case entirely and turned to Hogan and Hartson for assistance.

Large firms have been criticized for providing little support overall for public interest law, compared with billions of dollars in revenue they received each year. Also, because of the nature and extent of large firm's clientele, such firms often times find that a conflict of interest exists with potential public interest clients. In such cases, the interest of the paying client invariably prevails, and the law firm will refuse to represent the public interest position in that matter.

While some large law firms will accept costly and time consuming *pro bono* cases, typically large law firms are highly selective in their cases and provide little long-standing relief for their *pro bono* clients. They prefer to accept small cases, which are not likely to require much effort, but which allows them to be included on civic rosters as performing community service. For example, most law firms that accept "public interest" work would rather have their young associates handle a divorce or uninsured motorist case, than devote firm resources to an impact litigation case. Even when large corporate firms do accept public interest cases and win, most public interest attorneys will view their effort at tokenism which does not begin to undo the overall damage to society that they have done by supporting the status quo economic system rather than challenging it. For example, many public interest lawyers resent the fact that several large law firms defended redlining by banks (which prevented blacks from integrating neighborhoods), while claiming that they were for civil rights and perhaps even supporting a civil rights case or two. Furthermore, most large law firms established public interest programs not out of altruism, but because the brightest students from law schools were demanding that they do so or threatening to work elsewhere. Therefore, by participating in public interest cases, large law firms are able to attract law students with a public interest bend, train their associates on a few public interest cases, and then, once trained, move them to a profitable department within the firm. Ironically, even in firms with a commitment to public interest, associates believe that they risk their partnership chances by working too much on public interest cases, and therefore they may eschew the work.

Small Private Law Firms

Private law firms with a public interest orientation fill a void between non-profit organizations and corporate law firms. They have neither tax exempt status nor a dues-paying membership base which non-profit organizations have, nor do they enjoy significant income from well-endowed clients which corporate law firms have. Rather, these small private interest firms usually work on a fee for service basis, although the firms usually have standard lower rates than corporate firms, and they will oftentimes

41

further reduce their fees if the case interests them or the client is particularly forlorn. What makes this type of private law organization special is that:

> [t]he private public interest lawyer is primarily committed to providing representation to clients who could not normally afford to pay the going rates for legal services. This means, in practical terms, that he or she has made a decision to accept a limited income by charging rates which are substantially below those he or she could command from commercial clients.

Council for Public Interest Law, *Balancing the Scales,* at 134 (1975)

When working for a private client, these firms are more closely related to legal services than traditional public interest organizations. The individual clients these firms accept will usually have discreet complaints such as employment discrimination or other civil rights claims. They will have too many assets to qualify for a legal aid, but not enough to afford to pay going law firm rates.

Occasionally, the discreet injury cases will be expanded to include a large class. Numerous class action discrimination lawsuits have been initiated by one or several individuals approaching a small lawfirm to complain about discriminatory practices at work. The impact of the class action lawsuit will benefit thousands of workers, although this may not have been the complainant's goal when he or she approached the lawyer. Furthermore, even where a class action lawsuit is not filed, a discrete complaint can have a significant impact. For example, the lawfirm of Dobrovir & Gebhardt accepted what appeared to be a routine race discrimination case which involved a black employee of the U.S. Department of Agriculture. The employee complained that she was being discriminated against because she fought for the

Agriculture Department to provide more services to poor blacks. The attorney rapidly put the Department on the defensive, and held a news conference to publicize that his client was being fired for fighting racist Agriculture Department policies. The story became front page news across the country, and the subject of a presidential news conference. That case caused the Department to re-evaluate racial bias in distribution of its resources to blacks.

Most private publicly oriented law firms have taken on commercial clients by necessity. In most instances, the *pro bono* work is small. Furthermore small law firms are usually unable to accept large impact cases because of the drain on their financial resources and manpower which such cases require. The exception are law firms such are Harmon & Weiss in Washington, D.C., which represent public interest organizations exclusively. Because of their guaranteed clientele, and ability to call on lawyers within the organization to assist them, they have fewer financial concerns than other private law firms which would not have the guaranteed funding for large private cases.

Small law firms can handle large impact cases when they receive foundation funding or have a corporate component or other specialty which permits them to devote substantial resources to the effort. As one study noted:

> the private public interest law firm has a limited ability to represent clients who have no money at all, except in the narrow range of cases in which fee awards are possible. They cannot take on high risk cases or those massive cases where there is a substantial possibility that the client will run out of money before the case is resolved.

Balancing the Scales of Justice, supra, at 144.

43

Of all the publicly oriented attorneys' organizations, small private firms are in the most precarious situation in the 1980's. Competition for paying clients is intense, while winning attorney's fees and obtaining foundation support has become more difficult. (See "Attorneys Fees" discussion, *infra*). In summary small private law firms assist but will not be able to supplant the need for public interest organizations and large law firms.

Role of Public Interest Organizations—the Backbone of Public Interest Law

In the 1960's and 70's the world of public interest law as we now know it began. The birth of those organizations coincided with a heightened social consciousness raised by the civil rights movements. Books, such as Rachael Carson's *Silent Spring*, (1962) (regarding environmental pollution), Ralph Nader's *Unsafe at any Speed*, (1965) (automotive safety), Paul Erlich's *The Population Bomb* (1968) were particularly inspirational. News events also evoked moral outrage. Revelations that General Motors (the symbol of big business) had Ralph Nader spied upon for publishing *Unsafe at Any Speed*, government proposals to put a dam in the Grand Canyon which could have meant the destructions of one of the world's most cherished symbols (1966), the Santa Barbara oil spill with television pictures of birds paralyzed by oil (1969) and Watergate (1972-1974), had a profound impact upon society's changing moral philosophy.

Most organizations born during that period specialized in certain subject areas, especially environment, women's rights, minority rights and consumer issues. A few, such as the Center for Law and Social Policy and Center for Law in the Public Interest, became generalists. These organizations generally follow the same model: nonprofit corporation status with a prestigious board of directors and small salaried legal staff. Although each developed some techniques and approaches of its own, most followed the NAACP Legal Defense and Education Fund institutional model of:

(1) using a core of full-time salaried lawyers who perform much of the organizations legal work and supervise the legal work given to volunteer attorneys or counsels hired for special projects;

(2) accepting only impact litigation, not cases which are beneficial only to one individual;

(3) using litigation as a sword to further their organization's cause and to alter the way in which political and social institutions treat their cause;

(4) looking beyond foundations for financial support and forming a wide spread national membership base of small contributors;

(5) seeking all out victories when engaged in litigation involving statutory interpretation, but litigating constitutional issues incrementally using a "test case" approach;

(6) working with a network of private attorneys to implement judicial victories on a nationwide basis;

(7) attempting to collect attorneys fees for their efforts, so that they can rebuild their war chest for another battle.

During the 1960's, the first core of public interest law organizations to develop were the civil rights groups. Within the civil rights movement, the venerable NAACP Legal Defense and Education Fund (discussed *infra*) grew stronger during that period, increasing its legal staff over the next several years to 25 full-time attorneys, and 250 of the nations top lawyers formed the Lawyers Committee for Civil Rights Under Law ("LCCRUL") at President's Kennedy's request to bring the backing of the mainstream bar into the civil rights movement. Other minority rights groups such as The Mexican-American

45

Legal Defense Fund, Puerto Rican Legal Defense and Education Fund, Native American Rights Fund and National Center for Immigrants Rights were established and scored impressive victories for their memberships.

Environmental groups were the next major litigation area to rise after the civil rights movement of the early 60's. Numerous environmental statutes were passed during that period including the National Environmental Policy Act, Clean Air Act of 1970 and 1977, Federal Water Pollution Control Act amendments of 1972, Endangered Species Act of 1973, and the Toxic Substances Control Act of 1976, all of which required administrative enforcement. Environmentalists soon discovered that litigation against the EPA in particular was necessary to ensure that such laws were enforced. Long time environmental groups such as the Sierra Club (which established a legal defense fund in 1969) and the Wilderness Society were joined in that effort by a group of new litigation oriented groups such as the Environmental Defense Fund, Natural Resources Defense Council and Friends of the Earth.

Together and separately, these groups have caused the federal governmental to enforce the environmental laws. In the process they have established (through judicial decisions) important precedents for citizen suits against officials who were not enforcing the law, and standing for public interest organizations to sue on behalf of the environment. Furthermore, through skillful lobbying, environmentalists have procured through the statutory right to sue polluters directly ("citizens suit" or "private attorney general" provisions). For example, the Clean Air Act, 42 U.S.C. section 1857, permits citizen suits against the United States, states (to the extent permitted by the Eleventh Amendment of the Constitution), municipalities, corporations and individuals.

Consumer rights developed concurrently with environmentalism. Many of the environmental organizations that work on environmental issues, such as the Center for Law and Social Policy, Public Citizen Litigation Group and Trial Lawyers for Public Justice, also work on consumer issues.

The father of the modern consumer's movement is Ralph Nader. In 1970, Nader founded the Public Interest Research Group to pursue consumer oriented research, lobbying and litigation, using his personal funds and student contributions. In 1971 he established Public Citizen, Inc., as a permanent nationwide organization for consumer advocacy. Within the umbrella of public citizen he established six departments: Congress Watch, the Critical Mass Energy Project, the Health Research Group, Litigation Group, Tax Reform Research Group and Buyer's Up (a cooperative purchasing organization).

Several other organizations are active in pursuing consumer rights including Consumer's Union, Consumer Federation of America, Center for Auto Safety, and the Food Action Research Center. These organizations have played key roles in changing the fundamental basis in which regulations are enacted in the United States. Until such consumer groups emerged, regulatory agencies such as the Food and Drug Administration, Federal Trade Commission, National Highway Safety Administration and the Federal Communications Commission only had one party to listen to when setting regulations: those that they were suppose to regulate. Even when consumer groups emerged, regulators did not consider their input seriously until courts, beginning in 1966 with *Office of Communications of the United Church of Christ v. FCC*, 359 F.2d 994 (D.C. Cir. 1966), gave consumer groups standing to challenge agencies decisions and ordered agencies to weigh the consumer input. Consumer groups now, more than other public interest groups are more active administratively than judicially, because most consumer issues are within the jurisdiction of a federal agency to whom they must first look to for relief.

The last major public interest group to emerge from that era was the women's movement, whose litigation groups include the NOW Legal Defense and Educational Fund, ACLU-Women's Rights Project, National Abortion Rights League, National Women's Law Center (formally the Center for Law and Social Policy Women's Rights Project). These groups have traditionally litigated employment rights and abortion reform, and their efforts as counsel and *amicus* have resulted in the striking down of mandatory maternity leaves, opening up police and fire department jobs for women and equalizing workmen's compensation. The women's movements most famous victory is probably *Roe v. Wade*, in which the Supreme Court declared prohibitions on abortions to be unconstitutional. After that victory, states passed numerous laws to restrict a women's right to abortion. As they arise, those statutes are typically challenged at the trial level by the ACLU Women's Rights Project and the National Abortions Rights Action League, and those groups are joined through *amicus* briefs at later stages by other women's groups.

The newest concentration of women's litigation is insurance equalization. That litigation arises directly from the insurance industries opposition to the equal rights amendment, and their successful efforts to defeat it. The NOW Legal Defense and Education Fund is spearheading that effort, which they claim is an effort to end "one of the last vestiges of discrimination in an entire industry."

Role Models of Public Interest Groups

The American Civil Liberties Union

In 1920, the American Civil Liberties Union (ACLU) was formed based on three principles: protection of the First Amendment, guarantee of due process (e.g. no searches or seizures without a lawful warrant; protecting the right to a jury trial), and equal treatment under the law for all citizens.

The ACLU grew out of the National Civil Liberties Bureau which was founded in 1917 to protect the First Amendment rights of those who opposed U.S. intervention in World War I. Unlike other civil rights organizations such as the Civil Liberties Bureau, German Society of New York and the Freedman's Bureau (discussed *infra*) which were formed in reaction to the needs of a specific constituency, the ACLU was established to protect the constitutional rights of all citizens.

Initially, the ACLU had little organizational structure and engaged mostly in lobbying on behalf of the First Amendment. When it became involved in the litigation, usually to defend alleged draft evaders, its role was usually to file *amicus* briefs prepared by volunteer attorneys, rather than directly representing clients.

In the 1950s the ACLU changed its focus to organize units throughout the country. This became particularly important during that era because of widespread abuses of civil liberties at the local level resulting from McCarthyism. Each local has autonomy, although prior to filing an *amicus* brief in the Supreme Court they are expected to submit them to the national board to insure that it is consistent with National ACLU policy. In several instances, though, the National and local boards have split and filed *amicus* briefs on opposing sides of a

49

case. In addition, the national office, with a staff of 125, participates in its own projects independent of the locals, and runs special projects such as prisoner's rights, women's rights and immigrant's rights projects.

Unlike most legal aid litigation which focuses on individual problems, the ACLU focuses on issues which arise at the local level, but have national importance. The ACLU has particularly concentrated on First Amendment issues, such as protecting free speech rights of unpopular speakers or books, within the locality or state.

The ACLU has historically been unique because it defends principles regardless of the consequences. For example, the ACLU defended the rights of Nazis to march in Skokie, Illinois, a predominately Jewish community, despite the ACLU having a large Jewish membership. Furthermore, the ACLU is willing to support both sides of a war, in different battles. For example, the ACLU has participated in every major U.S. Supreme Court abortion case in support of a women's right to have an abortion, unfettered by governmental restraints. Yet in *Bering v. SHARE,* 106 Wash 2d 2121, 721 P. 2d 918 (1986), the ACLU filed an *amicus* brief in the Washington Supreme Court in support of anti-abortion activists who were ordered not to picket directly in front of an abortion clinic, or to use the words "kill" or "murder" in front of children while picketing. The ACLU reasoned that the issue in *Bering* was prior restraint on free speech, and was not inconsistent with also supporting abortion rights.

As a consequence of taking positions offensive to one or more of its constituent groups, the ACLU temporarily lost thousands of members, although apparently such losses have not been permanent. Few other litigation organizations follow the philosophy of defending principles rather than constituency groups as purely as does the ACLU.

The ACLU is also a pioneer in grassroots fundraising and organizing. Through its network of volunteers, it raises millions of dollars each year and receives thousands of hours of free legal services from volunteer attorneys. As some expected, the ACLU membership has swelled in the 1980s in the wake of the perceived assault on civil liberties by the Reagan Administration. At the same time, however, it finds itself focusing on many diverse issues, as it believes the Constitution is under assault from many directions.

The National Association for the Advancement of Colored People Legal Defense and Education Fund

The National Association of the Advancement of Colored People ("NAACP") was founded in 1909 (after a race riot in Springfield, Massachusetts), to serve as an educational and lobbying organization for Blacks. Not until 1915 did it become involved in litigation, when it filed an *amicus* brief in *Guinn v. United States,* 238 U.S. 347 (1915). In *Guinn,* the NAACP opposed an Oklahoma law which would allow anyone registered to vote before 1866 to remain registered (i.e. White persons) but required anybody not registered prior to that date (i.e. mostly Blacks) to pass a literacy test. In 1930, the NAACP received a sizable grant to develop "a comprehensive campaign against the major disabilities for which negroes suffer in American life — legal, political and economic." They hired Nathan Margold to develop the organization's legal policy, and his recommendations were adopted: they would fight the "separate but equal" doctrine through a carefully structured plan to incrementally secure decisions which would eventually lead to the repeal of that detested doctrine.

In 1939 the NAACP established a Legal Defense and Education Fund ("LDEF") as a separate entity. The legal defense fund went back to a strategy of an incremental (test case) litigation to develop rights. Blacks' earlier efforts to use that strategy failed disastrously, and resulted in *Plessy v. Ferguson*, 163 U.S. 537 (1896), which upheld the doctrine of "separate but equal." The LDEF was more successful with the test litigation strategy in part because it used top quality lawyers, (for example, United States Supreme Court Justice Thurgood Marshall joined the LDEF staff in 1936 and served as its chief legal officer from 1948 to 1961), litigated only egregious cases of discrimination and built on precedent of its own making. They won 34 of 37 Supreme Court cases in which they argued between 1939 and the 1954 *Brown* decision and each victory gave them precedent for the next case. Cases such as *Missouri ex rel. Gaines v. Canada*, 305 U.S. 337 (1938), *Sweat v. Painter*, 339 U.S. 629 (1950), and *McLaurin v. Oklahoma State Regents*, 339 U.S. 637 (1950), all challenges to the "equality" aspect of separate but equal doctrine, established that "separate but equal" did not result in equality. Those efforts resulted in the landmark decision in *Brown v. Board of Education,* 347 U.S. 483 (1954), which outlawed segregation in public schools and rapidly led to judicial repudiation of segregation.

Public Citizen Litigation Group

The Public Citizen Litigation Group began in 1972 as Ralph Nader's vehicle to sue the federal government. Within fifteen years, the Litigation Group has developed a nationwide clientele and has litigated numerous cases independently of the other Public Citizen groups. Its adversaries now include not only federal and state governments but corporations, banks, insurance companies, labor unions and their leaders, bar associations, doctors, lawyers and anyone else they perceive as having "power."

Increasingly, other organizations and individuals with significant legal problems have asked the litigation group for assistance, in some cases after defeats in lower Courts or before administrative agencies. The group, because of its small size and budget (approximately $600,000 in 1985) accepts few of the cases in which they are asked to participate. Among its criteria for selecting a case is that it must have the potential for significant impact, and that the matter is not in an area of the law in which there are many other groups with expertise or ability to fill at least a portion of the representational void (e.g. they usually do not accept environmental and civil rights cases).

As with many public interest groups during the 1980s, the Litigation Group has had to concentrate its efforts on making the Reagan administration obey the laws rather than simply trying to extend constitutional rights. Of particular concern to the Litigation Group has been public health and safety matters, and on keeping the government open. They have also concentated on battling the professions, particularly the legal profession and others on advertising restrictions, in an effort to make professionals' services more available and affordable, and protecting the rights of workers particularly in making their unions more democratic and open.

A common source for the Group's work is through its staff's daily activities such as reading newspapers. It was through reading the papers that they became involved in one of their most significant victories: their successful lawsuit to have the Gramm-Rudman Emergency Deficit Control Act of 1985, 2 U.S.C.A. §901 et. seq., declared unconstitutional. That case was developed through their interest and involvement in the matter when it was first being considered. Since they believed that the law was

53

unconstitutional from the time it was introduced into the Congress, they recommended that Congress enact a mechanism to give Congressman standing to challenge the Act and for prompt judicial review. After the Act passed, several Congressmen who opposed the measure retained the Litigation Group to sue on their behalf to have the Act declared unconstitutional. They prevailed in *Bowsher v. Synar,* _____ U.S. _____, 106 S. Ct. 3181 (1986) and as a consequence upset the entire federal budget making process.

The Litigation Group also handles the litigation for all of Public Citizen's component organizations, provides legal advice to all those organizations on matters pending before administrative agencies, and supplies testimony and expertise on legislative issues before Congress. The group has expanded to represent other public interest groups in Washington and elsewhere. Some of which, such as the Center for Auto Safety and Aviation Consumer Action Project, have been loosely affiliated with Public Citizen for several years.

Unlike most public interest groups which also pay poorly, the litigation group has slight turnover, with the average length of service being nine years. Furthermore, although the maximum salary is less than $43,000, the majority of its ten attorneys have more than ten years of experience, which would make them a partner in private practice.

The Big Three Environmental Organizations

When discussing environmental law, three organizations stand out: The Sierra Club Legal Defense Fund (SCLDF), Environmental Defense Fund (EDF) and Natural Resources Defense Council (NRDC). The three groups regularly consult on cases, and oftentimes join the others' lawsuits.

Each organization shares common interests but has a different structure and approach to litigation. SCLDF only engages in litigation, while the affiliated Sierra Club engages in lobbying activities. The EDF and NRDC on the other hand are more scientifically and less judicially oriented, with substantial staffs of scientists who regularly testify at administrative hearings and work with the incumbent administration for progressive energy and environmental laws. While the EDF has always been a membership organization, membership came as an after thought to the NRDC, in 1975, when the Supreme Court ruled that environmental organizations could only sue if they could allege that their members where injured — so the NRDC needed members for whom they could claim injury.

The three organizations get their cases in different ways. Much of the SCLDF litigation comes through the Sierra Club. EDF is the most community reactive organization, drawing much of their case load from inquiries from the community. The NRDC finds most of its own cases, and rarely takes a case based on community input. Because of the similarity of interest, they tend to draw on the same clientele — 40% of the membership overlaps among these organizations.

The Rise of Conservative Public Interest Groups

In 1935, the National Lawyers Committee of the American Liberty League was established as the first conservative "public interest" law firm. Its goal was to fight against New Deal legislation, and it disbanded when the group perceived that it could no longer have an impact.

Although conservative causes were well represented throughout history, conservatives did not form public interest organizations modeled after liberal organizations until the early 1970's. Led by former ABA president (and now Justice) Lewis Powell who declared:

> It is time for American business — which has demonstrated the greatest capability in all history to produce and influence consumers' decisions —to apply their great talents vigorously to the preservations of the system itself

business groups and companies, took heed and stepped up their presence in Washington, D.C. They quickly succeeded in killing liberal public interest groups' proposals, such as for a consumer protection agency and public financing of Congressional campaigns. Furthermore, after a string of liberal public interest litigation victories, conservative groups established their own non-profit litigation organizations such as the Washington Legal Foundation, Capital Legal Foundation, Mountain States Legal Foundation, Pacific Legal Foundation, Mid-Atlantic Legal Foundation and Gulf States Legal Foundation. The six Legal Foundations were established under an umbrella organization, the National Legal Center for the Public Interest. They have since each become independent, with their own charters.

Unlike most liberal public interest groups which have lost most foundation support, these conservative law groups enjoy considerable foundation support. Except in rare situations, they do not solicit for public contributions or membership.

The legal foundations will often times be seen on the same pleadings as liberal public interest groups — but rarely if ever on the same side. These groups will often times intervene in cases either to support the government's position against tightened government regulations (e.g., for maintaining lax effluent standards in clean water cases), or opposing the government for being too stringent with their controls (while in the same lawsuit the liberal public interest groups will sue to force the government to tighten its regulations.)

Another conservative public interest organization, the National Chamber Litigation Group, operates differently then the legal foundations. It is supported by business, solely to represent their economic interests. It does not claim to represent the broader public interest *per se*, although they maintain their groups' interest in a free economy is in the public interest.

Conservative public interest groups are significantly fewer than their liberal counterparts, but liberals agree that corporate trade associations are in reality conservative public interest groups also. Since 1969, these groups have substantially increased their presence before the Supreme Court.

Funding for Public Interest Organizations

During the 1960's and early 70's, foundations were responsible to a great extent for the birth and growth of public interest law. Of particular importance was the Ford Foundation, which in 1967 began donating millions of dollars to public interest causes. Initially, the funds went to established public interest organizations such as the NAACP/LDEF and LCCRUL. In 1970, the Foundation decided to become a principle source of support for public interest organizations, and went on to fund such fledgling public interest groups as the Center for Law and Social Policy, Public Advocates, Inc., Environmental Defense Fund, Sierra Club Legal Defense Fund, National Resources Defense Council, Women's Law Fund, Women's Rights Projects of the ACLU, Women's Legal Defense Fund, NOW Legal Defense and Education Fund, Legal Action Center of New York, National

Senior Citizens Law Center, Native American Rights Fund, Legal Action Center of New York, and the Puerto Rican Legal Defense and Education Fund.

The Ford Foundation was particularly instrumental in granting seed money to groups to establish public interest law firms to represent their interests. For example, in 1972 the Ford Foundation contributed $140,000 to help establish the Women's Law Fund, and in 1967 they gave 2.2 million dollars to help establish the Mexican American Legal Defense Fund. The size of that Ford Foundation grant is attributable to the finding that Mexican Americans were the "most disorganized and fragmented minority in American life. . .[who needed] a national organization to serve their social, economic and public needs." T. Castro, *Chicano Power* at 150 (1974).

In 1979 the public interest world was startled to hear that the Ford Foundation was withdrawing from general public interest litigation funding. Ford announced that year that it would terminate general funding for ten public interest law centers. As public interest organizations feared, this led to a general erosion of other foundation money. The drop came quickly. Between 1980 and 1981, the 350 largest foundations reduced their contributions for law related projects from 2.5% to 1% of their giving, a reduction of 18 million dollars. Foundation Center, *The Foundation Directory*, "Distribution of Grants by Subject Category" (1986). By 1983, that percentage dropped to .7%. Alliance for Justice, "Summary of Results" at 3 (unpublished, 1985). As one observer noted:

> The 80's may be destined to go down in public interest history as the decade of hard knocks. Federal funding disappeared, and foundation money failed to increase enough to make up the

difference. For some organizations, these cut-backs have been disastrous.

Searcy, "Marketing the Public Interest", 9 Pipe Line 1 (Spring, 1986).

To make up for the loses, public interest law organizations developed new fundraising strategies. One such successful strategy was used by the Center for Science in the Public Interest (CSPI). In 1982, CSPI decided to broaden its membership base by changing its newsletter "Nutrition Action" from an exclusively cause oriented publication to a "repository of nutrition information aimed at the average consumer." It then hired a direct mail consultant for $30,000 and sent out a test subscription solicitation. Encouraged by the results of the solicitation, they mailed 3.5 million subscription solicitations, using lists as varied as health food buyers to "Esquire Magazine" readers and targeted mailings on specific issues (e.g. deceptive food advertising) to potential members. By early 1986 the membership (which was included in the price of the subscription) went from 35,000 to 65,000, and they increased from 30% to 65% their income from membership dues and contributions.

Other methods of fundraising among public interest organizations include direct mail solicitations for membership, fundraisers and grants from other sources. As of 1983, one-third of public interest organizations income was from public support, approximately 10% came from state and local funding, corporate contributions and sales of material, and 17% came from the federal government. Summary of Results at 4-7. In 1983, corporations donated $3 million to public interest law organizations, which was .1% of their corporate giving. The federal government gave $18 million, or .036% of their grants and contracts to such organizations. Id. at 3.

59

While public interest organizations more than doubled their income between 1975 and 1983 (from $40 million to $105.4 million (cf. private law firms had gross receipts of $35.5 billion that year), the number of public interest law organizations during that time also increased, so that average income per group dropped 33% after inflation. As a consequence, many public interest law centers are now in precarious financial positions.

Funding is uneven among public interest organizations: in 1975, 60% of the public interest law organizations had income greater than $300,000 while 13% had incomes of over $900,000. The fifteen largest public interest law organizations received almost one-half of all the public interest funds. By 1983, 60% still had less than $300,000 income in 1975 dollars ($500,000 in 1983 dollars), and 11% of the largest groups kept up with inflation and earned $900,000 or more in 1975 dollars ($1.6 million or more in 1983 dollars). Ten public interest organizations (each with incomes of over $2 million in 1983) accounted for one-half of all public interest funding. By category, public interest organizations fared as follows: (adopted from Summary of Results at 4.)

How They Fared
After Inflation

Type of Group		(1975 - 1983) Primary Sources Of Income
Civil Rights and Minority Defense	Doubled their income (Since 1979)	Individual Contributions and Attorney Fees
Consumer	+ 11%	Individual Contributions and Memberships
Environmental	Quadrupled Their Income	Individual Contributions and Memberships
Poverty Law	Lost in Real Dollars	Federal Government Grants and Contracts to Provide Legal Services.
Women's Issues	Up 5 Times (from less than $1 million to greater than $5 million)	Primarily Foundations

Chapter 2

ON BEING A PUBLIC INTEREST LAWYER

A lot of my friends from college are already out
making money, with stability and they're not
eating peanut butter every night. If I wanted to
make money, there are many quicker and easier
ways to do it. I guess really that when I die, I want
somebody to write on my grave, "she cared".

Laura Erbs, law student and aspiring public interest attorney.
Quoted in Edwards, "The Ethical Dilemma: Serving the Public
Interest or Personal Interest," F Wash. U.L.S. Mag 8 (1985).

Becoming a public interest attorney is difficult as a
young lawyer, because of peer and law school pressure to
become a corporate lawyer, because public interest jobs
are extremely competitive to get, and those that are
available generally pay poorly.

Schools are generally blamed for the relative paucity of
public interest lawyers. The "elite model law school" has
created a "nondynamic industry, slow to change and
innovate." Law schools are accused of not teaching
students to look beyond the narrow cases which they
study, to the larger issues in contemporary affairs. In
short, the law schools are accused of serving the corporate
interests and the social, political and economic status
quo, and promoting the idea that high income at a
corporate law firm is the bellweather of success. That
perception is shared by the general bar:

> If an attorney does not go from law school to
> corporate law, some lawyers believe he may not
> be a first rate attorney and he probably cannot

handle what they perceive to be the more sophis-
ticated law which they practice.

A. Arriola & S. Wolinsky, *Public Interest Practice in Practice: the Law and Reality,* 34 Hastings L. J. 1207, 1209 (1983).

Another explanation, however, is that:

like its leaders, the [public interest] movement
has reached middle-age. The burst of youthful
energy that translated many of its goals into
public policy has given ways to a struggle to stem
erosion in both the movement's vitality and the
achievements of the 1970's.

Clark, "After a Decade of Doing Battle, Public Interest Groups Show Their Age," 28 Nat'l J. 1136 (1980).

To the lawyer where "me" comes first, public interest
law will be unattractive because of low pay. In 1983, 10%
of the public interest lawyers earned less than $15,000,
almost half the public interest attorneys earned $30,000
or less, 25% earned $31-40,000 and only 10% earned more
than $50,000. "Summary of Results" at 9. In 1985, the
starting salaries in New York for corporate law firms
averaged $39,000 and in Washington, D.C. the average
starting corporate salary was $36,000. The highest starting
corporate salary for those cities in 1986 was $70,000 and
$46,000 respectively. Not only are salaries for public
interest lawyers not comparable with private sector
salaries, but the bottom is increasing. In 1979, only 2% of
the public interest attorneys earned less than $10,000. In
1983, 10% made $10,000 or less (in 1979 dollars). While
money may be a problem, job satisfaction oftentimes
outweighs that problem. As one former corporate turned
public interest lawyer stated:

I couldn't be happier. There isn't a better job in

Washington, unless you call being a Supreme Court justice a "law job." To me, the saddest thing is people who get out of law school, go to work for a law firm, and never leave. The only things they change are their offices, homes and clubs.

Job security has also discouraged law students from entering public interest law. In 1982 to 1983, the Legal Services Corporation reduced its legal staff by 25%. In 1985 the Women Equity Action League laid off its legal staff because of lack of funds.

Nonetheless, demand for public interest law positions far exceeds the supply, and law students are increasingly showing interest in public interest law. According to the Alliance for Justice, public interest organizations which address civil rights and health and safety issues had 900 full-time attorney positions in 1985, divided among 159 public interest organizations. Although positions for attorneys are gradually increasing, public interest law organizations are spending a smaller percentage of their budget for attorneys. While the number of public interest organizations increased by 83% from 1975 to 1985 (from 87 to 159), the number of public interest organizations attorneys only increased by 33% from (600 to 900 positions). The trend among public interest groups is to bring in professionals such as scientists, editors and fundraisers, which allows the attorneys to concentrate more on legal issues, but reduces the demand these organizations have for attorneys.

Professionals now outnumber attorneys at public interest law organizations. To make matters worse for aspiring public interest attorneys, the trend among public interest organizations is to become smaller and more focused on specific issues. One-third of the public interest organizations employ only one or two attorneys, and one-third have three to five attorneys. The largest groups of attorneys are in the areas of civil rights (11 attorneys average), poverty law (11 attorneys average), and environmental law (9 attorneys average). Women's rights, gay rights, international and media organizations have much smaller legal staffs. The smaller the existing legal staff is, the smaller the likelihood is that they would hire an inexperienced attorney, since they do not have the resources to train that person.

The most recent study of public interest lawyers, performed ten years ago, found that public interest lawyers are more likely to be female, to have been in the top quarter of their law school class, to have participated in law review, to have served as a law clerk and to have graduated from a high-quality law school. They also tend to be younger, less experienced, and more liberal than the community at large. (According to one survey conducted by a conservative organization, only 4% of the public interest attorneys voted for President Ford in 1976, and only 2% voted for President Reagan in 1980.)

Characteristics which have been attributed to public interest lawyers include missionary zeal, camaraderie, self-sacrifice (low pay), independence from government and business, a sense of participating in democracy and substantial publicity for their participants and their work. These lawyers could probably go to most private interest law firms in the country, but they choose public interest law because it is difficult, exciting, challenging, and their personal role will be more important to a greater number of people than they can hope to achieve in private interest practice. Part of the attraction of public interest law is that it promotes the "purest" principles of American jurisprudence: the law will provide justice to all who have access to it.

Public interest lawyers perform basically the same tasks as private interest lawyers, but they are more issue oriented, i.e. they reject the concept that a "good" lawyer is one who will serve any client, regardless of how repugnant his cause is to the public welfare. Furthermore, they perform numerous tasks that private interest attorneys do not, such as organizing potential clients, educating them that they have legal remedies available to correct a perceived problem, and "alter[ing] social expectations of a client group" to prepare them for the upcoming battle. Public interest lawyers have a mission to solve perceived societal ills, rather than get rich. Therefore they can choose clients or classes of clients to represent with whom their interests coincide. Because they have clients with issues in which the lawyer believes, public interest lawyers find their work to be "exciting, stimulating and intensely rewarding."

Public interest cases tend to be more complex than most legal cases, and therefore the public interest attorney is confronted with more novel legal issues and public policy arguments than most attorneys. This situation creates the challenging and interesting work environment which public interest lawyers seek. Furthermore, because of the nature and impact of the cases, the courts' decisions are more often published and have a greater effect on the law than other cases. That aspect of public interest work gives the attorney the satisfaction of knowing that he has left his mark on the law for years to come. As Ralph Nader stated, "Public interest lawyers have the advantage of knowing that they are doing something useful with all that expensive legal education."

Together, the public interest lawyers and clients try to accomplish meaningful reform. They carefully weigh the options and how to achieve their ultimate goal, rather than just how to win their client's case on narrow grounds. For example, if the client loses at the trial stage, the public interest attorney will weigh not only the chance of success on appeal, but also what the risk is of losing the appeal and therefore setting a bad precedent. Appellants in private interest cases usually consider only the costs and benefits of an appeal without considering what the large scale impact would be if they lost.

Public interest attorneys must also wrestle with settling a strong case rather than taking the case to trial and establishing an important precedent. For a private interest litigant, the problem has an easy solution: settle. But the public interest attorney usually wants to establish favorable judicial precedent to have the maximum impact. (While settlements may be referred to as guidance in settling other cases, they have no precedential effect in other matters not inolving the same parties in the settled action.) The conflict arises from the attorney's professional goals versus his clients interest in immediate relief from his particular situation. The problem is particularly acute when the client has little education, is highly malleable, and is unable to independently choose among strategies.

A criticism of public interest attorneys has been that since market forces do not assure public interest clients a choice of attorneys, the public interest attorneys may serve their own interests - ideologically, publicly or financially, without fear of losing their client. However, the ABA Model of Rules Professional Conduct section 1.3 states that a lawyer is ethicly bound to serve diligently his client's interest, not his own.

The conflict between the attorney's and client's interest was recently exacerbated by the Supreme Court. In *Evans v. Jeff D.,* _____ U.S. _____, 106 S. Ct. 1531 (1986) the Court upheld the right of defendants to insist that public interest attorneys waive their fees as a condition for settlement. That decision puts the public interest attorney in a tenuous position, where he must choose between the interest of his clients (particularly if there is a serious situation which needs immediate correction) versus the attorney's monetary needs or goals. In *Jeff D.* the plaintiff's public interest attorney's were representing children who were confined in dangerous jail conditions in Idaho. As a condition for settlement, the State of Idaho insisted that the attorneys give up all their attorneys' fees. The attorneys were confronted with the choice of litigating the case potentially for years, during which time their juvenile clients would be subjected to life threatening conditions, or giving up their attorneys' fees. The attorneys chose to give up their fees but argued on appeal that they had done so under duress and therefore that the court should overturn that part of the agreement. The Supreme Court refused to do so. (The ABA Steering Committee on Ethics and Professional Responsibility supports the Courts decision because, according to its chairman, Robert O. Hetlage, "The ability of attorneys to settle cases should not be unduly hampered." 46 *National Law Journal* at 52 (Aug. 18, 1986)). It is estimated that requests for attorney's fees waivers are made in over one-half the civil rights cases litigated. *Jeff D.,* 106 S. Ct at 1544 n. 31.

Attorneys in public interest cases face another ethical problem which private interest lawyers oftentimes do not even consider: whether litigating the case presently would be good for an entire class, not just his client. If the case falls within an area of developing law, where others may be pursuing a plan to gradually change the law (e.g., how the NAACP gradually changed the "Separate but Equal Doctrine", discussed *supra*), it is important for the attorneys to consider "test case litigation" factors:

(1) Is the judicial system ready for a big change or just a little? (i.e. whether to bring the big case or several smaller

cases on the same issue);

(2) Are the alternatives, organize, educate or lobby, better suited to resolve the problem?;

(3) Is anyone working on the issue and do they have a strategy planned out? (usually attorneys within a particular public interest field have a network to discuss such issues, or will research cases or articles to identify other lawyers have worked on similar issues);

(4) Is the court where venue lies (i.e., where the case would be filed) likely to be receptive or hostile?;

(5) Is federal or state court a better forum for the case? (federal courts usually have a greater sensitivity to novel constitutional issues, they usually produce written and reported decisions, and the simplicity of the Federal Rules of Civil Procedures and liberal discovery make federal court appealing; however, state courts are sometimes more open to law reform in a particular geographical area, are more familiar with the trial record of individual lawyers, and the judges may give greater consideration to any state constitutional or statutory claims. Furthermore, some federal judges are particularly hostile to cases which could have been brought into state court (since it means more work for them) and jurisdictional disputes can eat up years of valuable time);

(6) To go for the "whole loaf" or "half a loaf?" If only half a loaf, then the law may stagnate for years; but if the attorney loses the issue by attempting to push the state of the law too quickly, then the cause may be set back for years;

(7) Will the client stay with the case through years of frustration, or will he prefer to negotiate or not raise novel issues, even if it means losing the entire precedent?

With all those considerations, some attorneys and organizations first choose the issue and strategy, and then find the client. The Supreme Court has approved of this

70

strategy for public interest cases. *Zauderer v. Office of Disciplinary Council,* ____ U.S. ____ 105 S. Ct. 2265 (1965), *in re Primus,* 436 U.S. 412 (1978); *NAACP v. Button,* 371 U.S. 415 (1963).

Chapter 3

LEGAL ISSUES COMMON IN PUBLIC INTEREST LAW

Attorney's Fees Statutes

One of the most important issues in public interest law is how to fund lawsuits, which are usually expensive, and can easily cost over $100,000. Generally, in the American litigation system, each party bears its own expenses to litigate an issue. The reason for this rule is:

> Since litigation is at best uncertain one should not be penalized for merely defending or prosecuting a lawsuit, and that the poor might be unjustly discouraged from instituting actions to vindicate their rights if the penalty for losing included the fees of their opponents' counsel.

Fleischmann Distilling Corp., v. Maier Brewing Co., 386 U.S. 714, 718 (1967).

The courts have created three exceptions to the American rule. The first situation arises when the defendant has acted in bad faith during the litigation, *see e.g. Newman v. Piggie Park Enterprise,* 390 U.S. 400, 422 (1968). But that rule is strictly applied and fees cannot be recovered for bad faith pre-litigation conduct which gave rise to the lawsuit, *Shimman v. International Union of Operating Engineers,* 744 F.2d 1226 (6th Cir. 1984) (en banc); *see also,* M. Schwartz, "Attorney's Fees Developments," Clearinghouse Review 36 (May 1985). The second judicially created exception is the "common benefit" exception, which spreads the cost of litigation to others who benefited from the action. For example, in *Mills v.*

Electric Auto - Lite, 396 U.S. 375 (1970), the court ordered the corporation to pay plaintiff's attorney's fees, on the grounds that the corporation benefited from the plaintiff's shareholder derivative action. In *Sprague v. Ticonic National Bank,* 307 U.S. 161 (1939), the court ordered other potential plaintiffs to contribute to plaintiff's suit because her suit had a *stare decisis* effect that entitled the others to recover from defendants' assets.

The "common benefit" doctrine was severely limited in *Alyeska Pipeline Service Co. v. Wilderness Society,* 421 U.S. 240 (1975) in which the United States Supreme Court barred awarding attorney's fees for plaintiffs who act as "private attorneys general" to serve the public interest:

> Since the approach taken by Congress to this issue has been to carve out specific exceptions to a general rule that federal courts cannot award attorneys' fees beyond the limits of 28 U.S.C. § 1923, those courts are not free to fashion drastic new rules with respect to the allowance of attorneys' fees to the prevailing party in federal litigation. . .
>
> *Id.* at 269.

Following *Alyeska,* Congress scurried to create or amend statutes to permit courts to award attorney's fees, particularly for civil rights, consumer and environmental lawsuits. Congress has enacted over 100 statutes which permit awarding of such fees, most notably under Title VII of the Civil Rights Act of 1964 which is the basis for a large percentage of civil rights claims. Congress also enacted legislation to permit recovery of attorney's fees from government entities. For example, states and municipalities became liable for attorney's fees under the Civil Rights Attorney's Fees Award Act of 1976, 42

U.S.C. Section 1988 which permits an award of attorney's fees for civil rights violations which are committed under color of state law.

The federal government became liable for attorney's fees under numerous statutes, including the Equal Access to Justice Act, which allows fees to be collected against the federal government in lawsuits where the government's position in the litigation or administrative proceeding was not "substantially justified." However, the Equal Access to Justice Act has proven to be a disappointment to those who believed it would open the federal treasury to plaintiffs who brought meritorious lawsuits against the federal government. The Department of Justice estimated that it would cost the government $100,000,000 in its first year (1980). During its first year and nine months only $2.5 million dollars was paid under that provision. It is unclear what impact that provision had on public interest law, since many lawsuits are brought under statutes which permit the prevailing party to recover attorney's fees without having to meet the stringent requirement of showing that the government lacked a "substantial basis" for its position.

The ability to recover attorney's fees has substantially altered the way public interest attorneys view cases. Small private law firms are able to take more cases where the plaintiff cannot pay, and public interest organizations can accept more large cases, with the expectation that they will win attorney's fees in at least some of those cases. Some public interest law firms rely on attorney's fees for 80% of their operating income, and therefore must win attorney's fee to survive. According to Ralph Nader, "it is now clear that attorneys can sustain themselves in cases where there is a statutory provision for attorney's fees . . . these statutes potentially could have profound effect on the evolution of substantive law

areas in which Congress has provided for attorney's fees."
The rationale for fee shifting in public interest cases is:

> the contingent fee arrangements that make legal
> services available to many victims of personal
> injuries would often not encourage lawyers to
> accept civil rights cases, which frequently involve
> substantial expenditures of time and effort, but
> produce only small monetary recoveries. . . "[F]ee
> awards have proved an essential remedy if private
> citizens are to have a meaningful opportunity to
> vindicate the important Congressional policies
> which these laws contain." . . .("The function of
> an award of attorney's fees is to encourage the
> bringing of meritorious civil rights claims which
> might otherwise be abondoned because of the
> financial imperatives surrounding the hiring of
> competent counsel").

> *City of Riverside v. Rivera,* _____ U.S. _____, 106 S. Ct. 2686, 2696
> (1986), quoting Senate Report at 2, U.S. Code Cong. & Admin.
> News 1976, p. 5910 and *Kerr v. Quinn,* 692 F.2d 875, 877 (2nd Cir.
> 1982).

Many public interest cases such as environmental,
consumer and Freedom of Information Act lawsuits have
an even more compelling reason for shifting attorney's
fees; since they oftentimes provide only for injunctive but
not monetary relief, there is no monetary award from
which the attorney can get a contingency fee. Another
compelling reason for fee shifting is that it unleashes
public interest forces to ensure that Congressional statutes
are enforced. Even the knowledge that citizen groups
have access to lawyers who will prosecute a case if
attorney's fees are available may be enough to deter
violation of the law.

Nonetheless, fee shifting has become mired in procedural problems. First, there is no guarantee that the attorney will not have to waive his fee as a condition of settlement. *Evans v. Jeff D.,* supra, 106 S. Ct. at 1531. Even if the case goes to trial, public interest attorneys risk losing a substantial portion of the fees they would otherwise be entitled to if they reject a defendant's settlement offer. Under Federal Rule of Civil Procedure 68, if a plaintiff rejects a defendant's settlement offer (also known as an "offer of judgment") and the final award is less than the settlement offer, the plaintiff cannot recover his "costs" which were incurred after the offer was made. In *Marek v. Chesny,* _____ U.S. _____, 105 S. Ct. 3012 (1985), the Supreme Court for the first time held that "costs" included attorney's fees. Therefore, if the plaintiff rejects the defendant's offer of judgment and final award (including attorney's fees) is less than defendant's offer, the plaintiff cannot recover for any attorney's fees which were incurred after the date of the settlement offer. (This is a double edged sword, however: it forces the defendant to make a reasonable offer early on if he wants to avoid future liability for attorney's fees, but it forces plaintiff's attorneys to settle earlier than they might like, particularly if the matter has substantial public importance and they want to litigate the matter to establish a precedent. For a good discussion of plaintiffs and defendants posturing after *Marek, see,* R. Gepp, "New Tactics in Civil Rights Actions", California Lawyer, 49 (April, 1986)). Finally, if there are fees to collect, collecting them can take years, yet in litigation against the government the prevailing party cannot obtain interest. *Library of Congress v. Shaw,* _____ U.S. _____, 106 S. Ct. 2957 (1976). As more than one attorney has bemoaned, "now, if you do win, after many years, against the odds, courts can cut your income by half or more, income that just barely kept you alive."

The rates at which public interest attorneys, including legal aid or other government funded litigation attorneys can collect, is the reasonable hourly rate usually charged by attorneys of equal experience in the area (although the experience may not be in the same subject area, i.e., public interest attorneys are entitled to recover at corporate attorney rates). For example, in *Blum v. Stenson,* 465 U.S. 886, (1984), the Court approved the fee application of a legal aid attorney with 1 1/2 years of experience at $95.00 an hour and another legal aid attorney with 3 1/2 years of experience at $105.00 an hour.

The amount of the attorney's fee is computed by multiplying the reasonable rate by a reasonable number of hours expended on the case. This is the "Lodestar figure." Until 1984, the courts could freely adjust this figure upwards or downwards based on twelve factors that were set out in *Johnson v. Georgia Highway Express, Inc.,* 488 F.2d 714 (1974): (1) the time and labor required; (2) the novelty and difficulty of the questions; (3) the skill requisite to perform the legal service properly; (4) the preclusion of other employment by the attorney due to acceptance of the case; (5) the customary fee; (6) whether the fee was fixed or contingent; (7) time limitations imposed by the client or the circumstances; (8) the amount involved and the results obtained; (9) the experience, reputation and ability of the attorneys; (10) the "undesirability" of the case; (11) the nature and length of the professional relationship with the client; and (12) awards in similar cases. Id., 488 F.2d at 717-719. In 1984, the Supreme Court in *Blum v. Stenson,* stated that the Lodestar Figure was presumed to be the reasonable fee to which counsel was entitled, and rejected several of the factors that *Johnson* held were acceptable reasons for increasing the Lodestar. (The factors "subsumed within the initial calculation" of the Lodestar were "novelty [and] complexities of the issues," "the special skills and experience of counsel," the "quality of representation," and the "results obtained.") Then in *Pennsylvania v. Delaware Valley Citizens Council,* _____ U.S. _____, 106 S. Ct. 3088 (1986), the Supreme Court further diminished attorney's fees recoveries by holding that upward adjustments of the Lodestar were permissible only in "rare" and "exceptional" cases, supported by both "specific evidence" on the record and detailed findings by the lower courts. The Court specifically held that the Lodestar Figure "thus adequately compensated the attorney and leaves very little room for enhancing the award based on his . . . performance." In short, the Lodestar Figure includes most if not all, the relevant factors comprising a "reasonable" attorney fee. (106 S. Ct. at 3098.)

On the bright side for public interest attorneys, the Supreme Court upheld the right of pubilc interest attorneys to collect attorney's fees that far exceed the amount of damages which the plaintiffs collect. In *Riverside v. Rivera,* _____ U.S. _____, 106 S. Ct. 2686 (1986), the Supreme Court on a 5 to 4 vote vindicated the ability of attorneys to collect fees in cases where there is an important constitutional right to litigate, but damages are relatively small. In that case, plaintiffs recovered $33,000 for violation of civil rights which occurred when policemen used tear gas to break up a Chicano family's bachelor party. The plaintiffs' attorneys received $245,000 in fees, which the Supreme Court upheld. As Justice Brennan (joined by three other Justices) stated:

> [a] rule that limits attorney's fees in civil rights cases to a proportion of the damages awarded would seriously undermine Congress' purpose in enacting Section 1988. Congress enacted Section 1988 specifically because it found that the private

market for legal services failed to provide many victims of civil rights violations with effective access to the judicial process. These victims ordinarily cannot afford to purchase legal services at the rates set by the private market.

Id. at 2695 (citation omitted)

Standing

Although public interest organizations seek to protect broad societal interests, the Supreme Court in recent years has stated its dislike for such cases:

The Judiciary seeks to avoid deciding questions of broad social import where no individual rights would be vindicated.

Gladstone Realtors v. Village of Bellwood, 441 U.S. 91, 99-100 (1979).

The mechanism the federal courts most often use to avoid deciding such issues is by denying standing to individuals or organizations in a case. "Standing" is a concept of the federal judiciary which permits only those with a genuine "case or controversy" to maintain an action in federal court. Its purpose is to ensure "concrete, adverseness which sharpens the presentation of issues upon which the court so largely depends for illumination of difficult constitutional questions." *Baker v. Carr,* 369 U.S. 204, (1962) (Brennan, J. concurring).

While standing is necessary for any action filed in federal court, in practice it is most often invoked when issues of public law and policy are at issue, usually when a private party seeks to compel some governmental action. In recent times, the Supreme Court has used standing as a basis to prevent important public interest issues from being decided, but it has done so in an inconsistent manner.

The modern rule for standing was established in *Association of Data Processing, Inc. v. Camp*, 397 U.S. 150, 153 (1970) which required (1) "injury in fact, economic or otherwise," and (2) that the interest sought to be protected by the complainant is arguably within the zone of interests to be protected or regulated by the statute or constitutional guarantee in question. As Justice Brennan stated in his dissenting opinion in that case "the zone of interest test was nothing more than a review of the case on its merits."

Standing is more important in public interest cases than in other cases because public interest litigation often time seeks injunctive or declaratory relief, rather than damages. For example, in *Laird v. Tatum,* 408 U.S. 1 (1972), the plaintiffs brought a class action lawsuit for an injunction to stop the United States Army from spying on civilians who were participating in lawful activities, such as organized protests against the Vietnam War. The plaintiffs claimed that the Army spying was having a "chilling effect" on the excercise of their Constitutional rights. On a 5-4 vote, the Supreme Court held that the plaintiffs did not have standing since they could not demonstrate a specific objective harm that anyone had suffered because of the Army's activity, or that anyone of the plaintiffs could show a threat of specific future harm.

In cases where monetary damages are requested, there is no question of standing on that claim, since an award of damages necessarily requires pleading and showing injury. If the plaintiff cannot prove damages, then the complaint is subject to a motion to dismiss for "failure to state a claim upon which relief can be granted," 28 U.S.C. section 12(b)(6). That motion is independent of alleging lack of standing. But in a complaint for damages and equitable relief (e.g. an injunction) the non-monetary matters are still subject to a standing challenge. For example, in *City of Los Angeles v. Lyons,* 461 U.S. 95 (1983), the plaintiff had been stopped by police officers and they, without provocation or legal justification, applied a choke-hold to him which caused him injury. He sued for monetary damages and also for injunctive relief, since the use of such choke-hold had caused over a dozen deaths in the city, and police used it disproportionately on minorities. The District Court enjoined further use of the choke-hold but the Supreme Court reversed, holding that the plaintiff did not have standing to seek injunctive relief because he could not show that he had a reasonable belief that he would encounter the same problem again. The Court therefore permitted the plaintiff to seek damages, but left the rest of the population of the city with no recourse through the federal court system.

The most important bar to standing in the federal system is that taxpayers cannot sue as taxpayers even if it means that there is nobody else who would have standing to challenge a clear constitutional violation. For example, Article one, Section 6 of the Constitution states:

> ". . . no person holding any office under the United States shall be a member of either House . . ."

This clause historically has been interpreted to mean that members of the Executive branch cannot also serve in the Congress. Certain citizens found that 130 members of Congress also held Commissions in the Armed Forces Reserves, which are a part of the Executive Branch. In *Schlesinger v. Reservists Committee to Stop the War*, 418 U.S. 208 (1974) the Court reasoned that "the only interest all citizens share in the claim advanced by respondents is one which presents injury in the abstract." Since the interest was one "shared by all citizens equally" the plaintiffs were unable to overcome the Court's requirement that they show specific injury and therefore the plaintiffs did not have standing.

Similarly, in *United States v. Richardson,* 418 U.S. 166 (1974), concerned taxpayers challenged the constitutionality of a statute permitting the CIA to forego a regular accounting to the public of its receipts and expenditures, despite the mandate of Article 1, Section 9, Clause 7 of the Constitution, which states:

> No money shall be drawn from the Treasury, but in consequence of appropriations made by law, and a regular statement and account of receipts and expenditures of all public money shall be published from time to time.

Again, the Court held that plaintiffs had only the generalized grievance "all members of the public" had, and held they had no standing. As one Justice Department official stated:

> it troubled the soul of a government under the rule of law for its citizens to be told: "Yes, the action challenged may well be illegal or unconstitutional, but no one in this vast country of over 200,000,000 persons can raise the issue in court."

While 49 of the 50 states allow taxpayer suits to prevent illegal expenditures of money, federal taxpayers have no recourse but to turn to the Congress to correct patently unconstitutional acts for which they cannot allege a specific injury.

In some instances, problems with standing can be overcome. In *Sierra Club v. Morton,* 405 U.S. 727 (1972), the Supreme Court held that the Sierra Club did not have standing to sue per se, but it could sue on behalf of its members who could allege that they "would be affected in any activities or pasttimes by the [developments which they sought to enjoin]." The Sierra Club simply amended its complaint to allege that the activity would injure its members enjoyment of the mountain, and pursued its lawsuit. (That case even had an added benefit by making some nonregular membership groups such as the Natural Resources Defense Council develop a regular membership so that they would have standing to sue.) The "injury in fact" requirement of *Sierra Club* requires slight allegations of harm: denial of access to information (e.g., under the National Environmental Policy Act or Freedom of Information Act) is sufficient to convey standing. In *United States v. Scrap(I),* 418 U.S. 669 (1973) the Supreme Court even held that a student organization whose members allegedly "used the forest, streams, mountains and other resources in the Washington area for camping, hiking, fishing and sightseeing and . . . [t]his use is disturbed by the adverse environmental impact caused by non-use of recyclable goods," had standing to challenge federal rates for shipment of recyclable material.

However, in the worst case, no realistic plaintiff will have standing. In *Warth v. Seldin*, 422 U.S. 490 (1975) the Court threw out a housing discrimination lawsuit which had already been in the courts for three and a half years, because, they held, none of the plaintiffs had standing. In *Warth*, the plaintiffs challenged the town zoning laws on the basis that they blatantly excluded low income people from living there. The plaintiffs were: nonresident minority individuals who alleged that they wanted to live in the town because of the challenged zoning laws; taxpayers from the neighboring city who said they were paying higher taxes to support public housing forced upon them by the defendants' exclusionary practices; a group with members who were residents in the town claiming that they were deprived of the benefits

84

of living in a racially and ethnically integrated community; and a home building association claiming lost profits for its members because of an inability to construct low and moderate income housing in the town. A sharply divided Supreme Court stated that none of the plaintiffs had standing because "a plaintiff who seeks to challenge exclusionary zoning practices must allege specific, concrete facts demonstrating that the challenged practices harm *him* and that he personally would benefit in a tangible way from the court's intervention." 422 U.S. at 508 (emphasis in original). As Justice Brennan stated in dissent, "the opinion, which tosses out almost every conceivable kind of plaintiff who could be injured by the activity claimed to be unconstitutional, can be explained only by an indefensible hostility to the claim on the merits." 422 U.S. at 520. After *Warth,* the Court expanded the "injury in fact" test to require that the plaintiff not only show injury to himself but that the injury could be redressed by a favorable decision. *Simon v. Eastern Kentucky Welfare Rights Organization,* 426 U.S. 26 (1976).

Environmentalists more than other public interest organizations have succeeded in meeting the courts strict public interest standing requirements. Perhaps the extreme was in *Duke Power Company v. Carolina Environmental Study Group,* 438 U.S. 59 (1978). In that case, an environmental group challenged the Price-Anderson Act which gave the defendant power company immunity from damages over a specific amount for any injuries arising from an accident at their nuclear power plant. The Court accepted the plaintiffs' argument that if they were being adversely affected by living near a potential nuclear power plant, and that if they prevailed in having the Price-Anderson Act declared unconstitutional, it would not be built. The Court held that the plaintiffs had standing even though the likelihood of injury and the likelihood of success for redress if they prevailed were highly speculative.

To ameliorate standing problems, Congress has in some situations the power to grant standing to plaintiffs. For example, in *Havens Realty Corp. v. Coleman,* 455 U.S. 363, (1982) the plaintiff accused the defendant of refusing to rent to blacks in violation of the Fair Housing Act of 1968. The Court gave standing to individuals who never intended to rent from the defendant but merely acted as "testers" to determine whether the defendant would rent to them. The Court noted that the Act prohibited making an unlawful or false representation about the availability of a dwelling on account of race, color, religion, or national origin. The Court concluded that the statute conferred on all persons "a legal right to truthful information about available housing" and therefore the testers who had been lied to had standing.

In summary, standing is a complex issue which even the Supreme Court has had difficulty grasping. Public interest lawsuits for damages will withstand a challenge at least as to monetary damages which are requested (provided there is a private right of action, discussed *infra*). Furthermore, Congress can to a great degree confer standing on plaintiffs, and are doing so with increasing frequency. (Most statutes which specifically confer standing also provide for attorney's fees.) Finally, it is important for public interest litigants to include as many types of plaintiffs as possible in a lawsuit who can allege a specific injury and benefit from redress of that injury.

Implied Rights of Action

Another issue public interest plaintiffs face is whether the statute which is the basis of their lawsuit confers on them explicitly or implicitly the right to sue in federal court. As courts of limited jurisdiction, federal courts may not exercise their judicial powers without an express or implied basis on which to hear the case. Congress has enacted two statutes that the courts have interpreted to provide express rights of actions against many state and federal defendants. Section 702 of the Administrative Procedure Act states:

> A person suffering a legal wrong because of agency action or adversely affected or aggrieved by agency action within the meaning of a relevant statute, is entitled to judicial review thereof.

The Supreme Court has interpreted this section to provide a right of action against federal administrative agencies except where another statute precludes judicial review or the "agency action is committed to agency discretion by law." Generally these exceptions have been strictly construed thereby liberally allowing suits against the federal government.

Plaintiffs may also sue the federal government under the Federal Torts Claim Act 28 U.S.C. Section 2672 which states:

> The United States shall be liable, respecting the provisions of this Title relating to Tort Claims, in the same manner and to the same extent as a private individual under like circumstances, but shall not be liable for interest prior to judgment or for punitive damages.

That Act effectively waives the Federal government's sovereign immunity, but has two distinct disadvantages: punitive damages cannot be recovered against the federal government and attorney's fees are limited to 25% of the amount the plaintiff is awarded if the case goes to trial or

20% if the case is settled prior to trial. That provision may make it more difficult for plaintiffs to find attorneys to handle such cases.

Elsewhere in the Federal Torts Claim Act arises three exceptions to the waiver of immunity: if the action was a "discretionary function" of any federal agency or employee; if the conduct is not deemed to be a negligent or wrongful act or omission; or it is the tort of "misrepresentation." The first exemption, for discretionary functions, pertains only to policy making decisions, and even if the decision is deemed to be discretionary, the Court may invoke it equitable powers and enjoin the policy decision if it is contrary to the law. (In such a case, however, the plaintiff will not be able to recover monetary damages for such a suit). The second statutory exemption for negligent or wrongful act, has also proved troubling. For example in *Laird v. Nelms*, 406 U.S. 797 (1972), the Supreme Court held that the government could not be sued under the Federal Torts Claim Act for damages caused from sonic booms of military airplanes, based on the theory of strict liability. Therefore, unless fault can be shown, the government is exempt from claims. The third statutory exemption, for misrepresentation, has proven troublesome in some limited situations. For example, in *Mizokmi v. United States*, 414 F.2d 1375 (Ct. Cl. 1969) the plaintiff's spinach was seized for contamination with the pesticide heptachlor. It was later admitted that the original tests were in error and the spinach was uncontaminated. Nonetheless, the Court held that because it was an act of misrepresentation, the government was not liable.

There are two major judicially crafted exceptions to federal waiver of sovereign immunity: for violation of constitutional rights by federal employees and injury to servicemen. In the first situation, citizens do not have the right to sue the federal government for monetary damages arising from a violation of their constitutional rights. However, in *Bivens v. Six Unknown Federal Narcotics Agents*, 403 U.S. 388 (1971), the Supreme Court established that federal employees who act under the color of the law may be liable personally for such violations. In *Bivens*, the six narcotics agents went to the plaintiff's house, entered, handcuffed him, threatened to arrest his entire family, searched his house "from stem to stern," brought him to the police station, booked and strip searched him, all without cause. The Court held that the agents could be held personally liable for violating the plaintiff's fourth amendment rights, but also held that the federal government, because of its sovereign immunity, could not be held liable. *Bivens* has been limited to situations where the discretionary conduct violates a "clearly established" statutory or constitutional right of which a reasonalble person would have known. *Harlow v. Fitzgerald*, 457 U.S. 800 (1982).

The other major exception arises from military service. Under the doctrine known as the "Feres Doctrine," (named after the case *Feres v. United States*, 340 U.S. 135 (1950)), neither service men nor their estate may sue for any injuries which "arise out of or in the course of activity incident to service." The Supreme Court explained:

> "In the last analysis *Feres* seems best explained by the 'peculiar and special' relationship of the soldier to his superiors, the effects of the maintenance of such suits undisciplined, and the extreme results that might obtain if suits under the [Federal] Torts Claim Act were allowed for negligent orders given or negligent acts committed in the course of military duty."

United States v. Muniz, 374 U.S. 150, 162 (1963) quoting *United States v. Brown*, 348 U.S. 110, 112 (1954).

It is possible however that estates of service men killed in the line of duty or under the direction of civil authorities (i.e., civilian air traffic controllers) may be able to sue the civilian agencies by invoking the Federal Torts Claims Act. *Johnson v. United States,* 779 F.2d 1492 (11th Cir. 1985). (en banc)

Where sovereign immunity has not been specifically waived, the plaintiffs must look to the statute to see whether it expressly or implicitly grants a "private right of action" to sue. As stated above, numerous federal statutes grant such rights including over 100 that permit recovery of attorney's fees for exercising those rights. The interpretation of statutes to see whether they grant a private right of action is where the philosophical difference between liberals and conservatives can have a profound impact on the operation of the Court system for the next several decades. Under a "strict constructionist" (conservative) approach, unless the statute specifically grants the private right of action, a citizen does not have a right to sue to enforce the statute. The effect of this approach is that it "closes the courthouse door to aggrieved persons seeking judicial relief for violations of rights created by Congress" and as a consequence, it effectively immunizes private businesses and other regulated entities from a judicial review of their noncompliance with regulatory requirements. The severest consequences of the strict constructionist position fall upon minorities and the poor.

> . . .Lacking the political or economic power to remedy systematic abuses of their rights before Congress or the responsible administrative agencies, minorities and the poor turn to the Courts for legal protection. By closing the courthouse doors, the strict constructionist will leave these groups without a responsible, peaceful

forum to redress their grievances, and therefore without remedies for violations of rights created by Congress.

S. Romfeldt, "Implying Rights of Action for Minorities and the Poor Through Presumptions of Legislative Intent", 34 Hasting L.J. 969 (May/July 1983).

The modern test for whether a private right of action should be implied was set forth in *Court v. Ash,* 422 U.S. 66, 78 (1975) where the Supreme Court established four criteria:

First, is the plaintiff "one of the class for whose especial benefit the statute was enacted,". . . that is, does the statute create a federal right in favor of the plaintiff? Second, is there any indication of legislative intent, explicit or implicit, either to create such a remedy or to deny one? . . . Third, is it consistent with the underlying purposes of the legislative scheme to imply such a remedy for the plaintiff? . . . And finally, is the cause of action one traditionally relegated to state law, in an area basically the concern of the states, so that it would be inappropriate to infer a cause of action based solely on federal law? [citation omitted]

Of particular concern to potential public interest plaintiffs is whether they qualify as the special class for whom the statute was enacted. In *California v. Sierra Club*, 451 U.S. 287 (1981), the Court held that the Rivers and Harbors Appropriation Act of 1899, which prohibited unauthorized obstruction of navigable waters, was not enacted for the environmentalist/plaintiffs benefit since the Court deemed it "a general ban which carries with it no implication of an intent to confer rights on a particular class or persons." That is, just because environmentalists are concerned about the issues, and may even appreciate

91

the river more than others, they could not sue to enforce that Act.

Still unresolved is whether potential beneficiaries, such as low income tenants who are eligible for public housing, qualify as the special group to sue for enforcement of entitlement programs. For example, could a low income person, entitled to public housing, sue to prevent the government from closing down a nearby low income housing project in which he could potentially live. Also unresolved is the issue of whether potential beneficiaries can enforce their rights where third parties are involved. For example, the Davis-Bacon Act requires that contractors working on federal jobs pay the prevailing wage. A federal statute requires that such provision be put in all relevant construction contracts. Yet the Court in *University Research Association v. Coutu,* 450 U.S. 754 (1981), indicated that potential laborers had no private cause of action to force the Secretary of Labor to put that provision in the construction contract.

Despite the Supreme Court's strict construction leanings, civil rights groups have fared well with the Court on issues involving implied rights of actions. The Court has held that individual voters had an implied right to challenge local voting enactments under Section 5 of the Voting Rights Act of 1965, an implied right of action under Title 6 of the Civil Rights Act of 1964 to force a school district receiving federal funds to comply with regulations prohibiting recipients from discriminating on the basis of race, and an implied a right of action for a plaintiff under Title 9 of the Civil Rights Act prohibiting sex discrimination.

Consumer and environmental groups have not fared as well. In several instances, where the Court has found that Congress has established alternative judicial and administrative remedies, if the alternative remedies are comprehensive, the Court will generally deny implied rights of action for the plaintiff even when he falls within the special class to be protected. For example, in *National Railroad Passenger Corp. (AMTRAK) v. National Association of Railway Passengers*, 414 U.S. 453 (1973), the court held that because the Rail Passenger Service Act of 1970 expressly provided for a cause of action enforceable only by the Attorney General, that there could be no implied right of action for consumers. In *Middlesex County Sewage Authorities v. National Clammers Association*, 453 U.S. 1 (1981), the plaintiff fishing organizations sought to enjoin the federal government from polluting the ocean in violation of the Federal Water Pollution Control Act. That Act contains "civil and criminal" penalties, but also contains "unusually elaborate" enforcement procedures for public and private suits. The Court held that Congress could not have intended the Act to permit an implied right of action for plaintiffs to sue in court, when they had set up such an elaborate administrative procedure prior to filing a lawsuit. However, as one Justice exhorted:

> As a general matter, it is clear that the fact that the federal administrative agency has the power to oversee a cooperative state-federal venture, does not mean that Congress intended such oversight to be the exclusive remedy for enforcing statutory rights. This Court is most reluctant to assume Congress has closed the avenue of effective judicial review to those individuals most directly affected by the administration of its programs even if the agency has a statutory power to cut off federal funds for noncompliance.

Pennhurst State Schools v. Halterman, 451 U.S. 1, 52 (1981), (White, J. dissenting), quoting *Rosado v. Wyman*, 392 U.S. 397, 420 (1970).

Thus, public interest plaintiffs can argue that if the administrative remedy is not comprehensive or is inadequate, then there should be no presumption of exclusivity and a private right of action can be inferred. Indeed:

> This Court has sometimes refused to imply private rights of action where administrative or like remedies are available . . . but it has never withheld a private remedy when the statute explicitly confers a benefit on a class of persons and where it does not assure those persons the ability to activate and participate in the administrative process contemplated by the statute.

Canon v. University of Chicago, 441 U.S. 677, 709 n. 41 (1979).

Limitations on Lawsuits Against States

Citizen suits against a state in federal court is limited by the Eleventh Amendment which states:

> The Judicial Power of the United States shall not be construed to extend to any suit in law or equity commenced or prosecuted against one of the United States by citizens of another state, or by citizens or subjects of a foreign state.

For almost a hundred years that Amendment lay dormant, until the Supreme Court reinvigorated it beginning in the mid-1970s under the rediscovered concept of "state's rights." Since the Court's decision in *Ex-parte Young,* 209 U.S. 123 (1908), it was thought that the Eleventh Amendment did not bar suits by a citizen of the state against his state for violation of federal law. The Supreme Court in *Edelman v. Jordan,* 415 U.S. 651 (1974) took a decidedly more restrictive approach, and

94

held that *Ex-Parte Young* referred only to lawsuits against a state for prospective payments. In *Edelman*, the plaintiffs were suing for welfare payments which the state improperly failed to pay. The Supreme Court held that federal judicial power extended only to ordering the state to make future payments, but they could not be ordered to make retrospective payments because it would be too disruptive to the state treasury. The court recognized that they were in effect overruling twenty-eight prior Supreme Court cases which held otherwise, but in a bold statement of judicial activism, the conservative Justices on the Court stated "since we deal with a constitutional question, we are less constrained by the principle of *stare decisis* than we are in other areas of the law." 415 U.S. at 671.

In a further blow to efforts to obtain relief from states in federal court, the Supreme Court also stated that waiver of Eleventh Amendment sovereign immunity will be strictly construed, so that if a statute is not clear on its face that the state may be sued, the Eleventh Amendment will be invoked to protect it. The full implications of *Edelman* have not yet been realized. Since that case, the Court has held that even requiring a state to send out notice that they had violated federal law in denying certain welfare benefits, and that retroactive payments were possibly available through a state administrative or judicial action, could not be mandated by a federal court. Without such notice, few of the potential beneficiaries would be expected to recognize the rights which the federal action had conferred upon them. Nonetheless, the Court reasoned that such notice would cost the state money and therefore is barred by the eleventh amendment. *Green v. Mansour, Director, Michigan Department of Social Services, _____ U.S. _____, 106 S.Ct. 423 (1986).*

Although states can submit to waiving sovereign immunity, the Supreme Court construes such waivers narrowly. For example, in *Atascadero State Hospital v. Scanlon,* _____ U.S. _____, 105 S.Ct. 3142 (1985), an unsuccessful applicant for a position with the state hospital brought suit against the state for violations of the federal Rehabilitation Act. The plaintiff sought compensatory damages, injunctive and declaratory relief. The plaintiff argued that by receiving federal funds, the state had waived its Eleventh Amendment immunity, thereby permitting the state to receive federal funds but not subjecting itself to federal court jurisdiction to enforce the proper spending of those funds. As Justice Brennan noted in his dissent:

> In consequence, the Court has put the Federal Judiciary in the unseemly position of exempting the states from compliance with laws that bind every other legal actor in our nation.

The full impact of *Alterscadero* has yet to be seen, but commentators have worried that it could prevent enforcement of numerous federal statutes which predicate enforcement on the citizen's ability to sue because the state accepts federal funds and thereby waives its immunity. Furthermore, declaratory judgment and injunctions are traditionally thought of as prospective remedies. Yet, the court held that the plaintiff in *Alterscadero* was barred from this type of relief.

Plaintiff's suing the state would do well to consider suing in state court rather than federal court. Every state has waived sovereign immunity to some extent, if not entirely. The disadvantage, of course, is that sometimes state courts are more parochial and less willing to grant rights to plaintiffs, particularly monetary rights against the judge's own state. Furthermore, where the plaintiff seeks relief against the state on both federal and state law grounds, he must either litigate the federal and state

96

claims in federal and state courts respectively, or submit the entire matter to the state court. This remarkable result was achieved in *Pennhurst State School and Hospital v. Halterman*, 465 U.S. 89 (1984) where the court overruled over twenty cases to reach its decision. That decision also has far reaching consequences because civil rights attorneys often used state laws and regulations to remedy oppressive conditions in such institutions as jails, prisons and mental hospitals. Shortly after *Pennhurst* was decided, the United States Justice Department disavowed consent degrees previously negotiated based on state law, stating that the federal government no longer had a role in enforcing those laws.

Despite increasing restrictions on the ability of citizens to sue states, the Supreme Court has left intact the ability of plaintiffs to sue states under Section 1983 of the Civil Rights Act of 1899, which prohibits violations of civil rights under color of state law. However, Section 1983 does not apply where the suit involves state enforcement of federal law (e.g., failure to make welfare payments as required by law).

Appendix I
PUBLIC INTEREST LAW ORGANIZATIONS

Introduction

This directory was compiled from information received during the course of a survey of public interest law centers conducted by the Alliance for Justice in 1980. It includes non-profit organizations devoting some share of their programs to providing legal representation for otherwise-unrepresented interests, in court and administrative agency proceedings, involving questions of public policy.

The directory has three sections:
1) An alphabetical listing of the groups, including addresses, telephone numbers, and the location of any branch offices;
2) An index of the groups arranged according to their programmatic emphasis;
3) A geographical index by the state in which the groups' main offices are located.

It is advisable to contact the organizations directly for a more detailed description of their current activities and interests.

ADVOCACY CENTER FOR THE ELDERLY AND DISABLED, 1001 Howard Avenue, Suite 300 A, New Orleans, Louisiana 70013. Phone: 504-522-2337.
Branches: Shreveport and Alexandria, Louisiana. (Formerly Louisiana Center for the Public Interest; Advocates for the Developmentally Disabled)
ADVOCACY, INC., 7700 Chevy Chase Drive, Su. 300, Austin, Texas 78752. Phone: 512-475-5543.
ADVOCATES FOR BASIC LEGAL EQUALITY, INC., 740 Spitzer Building, Toledo, Ohio 43604. Phone: 419-255-0814. Branches: Fremont, Findlay, Defiance.
ADVOCATES FOR CHILDREN OF NEW YORK, 24-16 Bridge Plaza South, Long Island City, New York 11101. Phone: 718-729-8866. (formerly National Committee for Sexual Civil Liberties) Branch: Princeton, New Jersey
AMERICAN ASSOCIATION FOR PERSONAL PRIVACY, 1782 Pacific Avenue, San Francisco, California 94109. Phone: 415-474-8408 (formerly National Committee for Sexual Civil Liberties) Branch: Princeton, New Jersey.

AMERICAN CIVIL LIBERTIES UNION/ACLU FOUNDATION, 132 West 43rd Street, New York, New York 10017. Phone: 212-944-9800. Regional offices: Atlanta, Georgia; Denver, Colorado; Legislative Office: Washington, D.C. Fifty state and local affiliates throughout the country.

ACLU PROJECT ON NATIONAL SECURITY AND CIVIL LIBERTIES, 122 Maryland Avenue, NE, Washington, DC 20002. Phone: 202-544-5380.

AMERICAN COUNCIL OF THE BLIND, 1211 Connecticut Avenue, NW, Su. 506, Washington, DC 20036. Phone: 202-833-1251.

APPALACHIAN RESEARCH AND DEFENSE FUND, 1116-B Kanawha Boulevard East, Charleston, West Virginia 25301. Phone: 304-344-9687. Braches: Beckley, Fayetteville, Hamline, Logan, Pineville, Princeton, Welch, and Williamson, West Virginia.

ARIZONA CENTER FOR LAW IN THE PUBLIC INTEREST, 112 North Fifth Avenue, Phoenix, Arizona 85003. Phone: 602-252-4904. Branch: Tuscon, Arizona.

ASIAN AMERICAN LEGAL DEFENSE AND EDUCATION FUND, 350 Broadway, Suite 308, New York, New York 10013. Phone: 212-966-5932.

ASIAN LAW CAUCUS, 1322 Webster, Suite 210, Oakland, California 94612. Phone: 415-835-1474. Branch: San Francisco, California.

AVIATION CONSUMER ACTION PROJECT, P.O. Box 19029, 1346 Connecticut Avenue, NW, Suite 717, Washington, DC 20036. Phone: 202-223-4498.

BAY AREA CENTER FOR LAW AND THE DEAF, 125 Parrott, San Leandro, California 94577. Phone: 415-895-1610

BUSINESS AND PROFESSIONAL PEOPLE FOR THE PUBLIC INTEREST (BPI), 109 North Dearborn Street, Suite 1300, Chicago, Illinois 60602. Phone: 312-641-5570.

CAPITAL LEGAL FOUNDATION, 700 E Street, SE, Washington, DC 20003. Phone: 202-546-5533.

CAROLINA LEGAL ASSISTANCE, Mental Disability Law Project, Box 2446, Raleigh, North Carolina 27602. Phone: 919-834-0723.

CENTER FOR APPLIED LEGAL STUDIES, Georgetown University Law Center, 605 G Street, NW, Washington, DC 20001. Phone: 202-625-8311.

CENTER FOR AUTO SAFETY, 2001 S Street, NW, Su. 328 Washington, DC 20009. Phone: 202-828-7700.

CENTER FOR CONSTITUTIONAL RIGHTS, 853 Broadway, 14th Floor, New York, New York 10003. Phone: 212-674-3303. Branch: Greenville, Mississippi.

CENTER FOR LAW AND EDUCATION, 3rd floor, Six Appian Way, Cambridge, Massachusetts 02138. Phone: 617-495-4666.

CENTER FOR LAW AND HEALTH SCIENCE, c/o Professor H. Beyer, Boston University Law School, 765 Commonwealth Avenue, Boston, Massachusetts 02215. Phone: 617-353-2904.

CENTER FOR LAW AND SOCIAL POLICY, 1616 P St., NW, 3rd floor, Wash., DC 20036. Phone: 202-328-5140.

CENTER FOR LAW IN THE PUBLIC INTEREST, 10951 W. Pico Boulevard, Los Angeles, California 90064. Phone: 213-470-3000. Washington Office: 1575 I Street, NW, Washington, DC 20005. Phone: 202-371-0199.

CENTER FOR PUBLIC REPRESENTATION, 520 University Avenue, Madison, Wisconsin, 53703. Phone: 608-251-4008.

CENTER FOR RURAL AFFAIRS, P.O. Box 405, Walthill, Nebraska 68067. Phone: 402-846-5428 (formerly Small Farm Advocacy Project) Branch: Hartington, Nebraska.

CENTER FOR SCIENCE IN THE PUBLIC INTEREST, 1501 16th Street, NW, Washington, DC 20036. Phone: 202-332-9110.

CENTER ON SOCIAL WELFARE POLICY AND LAW, 95 Madison Avenue, Room 701, New York, New York 10016. Phone: 212-679-3709. Branch: Washington, DC.

CHICAGO LAWYERS' COMMITTEE FOR CIVIL RIGHTS UNDER LAW, INC. 220 South State Street, Suite 300, Chicago, Illinois 60604. Phone: 312-939-5797.

CHICANO EDUCATION PROJECT, 1410 Grant Street, Suite B104, Denver, Colorado 80204. Phone: 303-830-1052. Branches: San Luis Valley Center, Colorado; Ignacio, Colorado; Arkansas Valley, Rocky Ford, Arkansas.

CHILDREN'S DEFENSE FUND, 122 C Street, NW, Washington, DC 20008. Phone: 202-628-8787. Branch: Jackson, Mississippi; Columbus, Ohio.

CHILDREN'S RIGHTS GROUP, 693 Mission Street, Suite 600, San Francisco, California 94105. Phone: 415-495-7283. Branches: Santa Rosa, and Los Angeles, California; Helena, Montana; Denver, Colorado; Pierre, South Dakota.

CHILDREN'S RIGHTS PROJECT OF THE ACLU, 132 West 43rd Street, New York, New York 10017. Phone: 212-944-9800.

CITIZENS COMMUNICATION CENTER, 600 New Jersey Avenue, NW, Washington, DC 20001. Phone: 202-624-8047 or 8057.

COLORADO COALITION OF LEGAL SERVICES PROGRAMS, 770 Grant Street, Suite 206, Denver, Colorado 80203. Phone: 303-830-1551.

COLORADO LAWYERS' COMMITTEE, 1441 18th Street, Suite 50, Denver, Colorado 80202. Phone: 303-297-3115.

COMMUNICATIONS MEDIA CENTER, New York Law School, 57 Worth Street, New York 10013. Phone: 212-966-2053.

COMMUNITY HEALTH LAW PROJECT, 55 Washington Street, East Orange, New Jersey 07017. Phone: 201-672-6050. Branches: Elizabeth, Camden, Trenton New Jersey.

CONNECTICUT FUND FOR THE ENVIRONMENT, 152 Temple Street, Suite 412, New Haven, Connecticut 06510. Phone: 203-787-0646. Branch: New Haven, Connecticut.

CONSERVATION LAW FOUNDATION OF NEW ENGLAND, INC., Three Joy Street, Boston, Massachusetts 02108. Phone: 617-742-2540.

CONSTITUTION LITIGATION CLINIC, Rutgers University Law School, 15 Washington Street, Newark, New Jersey 07102. Phone: 201-648-5687.

CONSUMERS UNION, Litigation Office, 2001 S Street, NW, Washington, DC 20009. Phone: 202-462-6262. Branches: San Francisco, California; Austin, Texas; Mount Vernon, New York.

DISABILITY RIGHTS CENTER, 1346 Connecticut Avenue, NW, Washington, DC 20036, Suite 1124. Phone: 202-223-3304.

DISABILITY RIGHTS EDUCATION AND DEFENSE FUND, INC., 2032 San Pablo Avenue, Berkeley, California 94702. Phone: 415-644-2555. TDD: 415-644-2629. Branch: Washington, DC.

EDUCATION LAW CENTER, INC., 225 South 15th Street, Suite 2100, Philadelphia, Pennsylvania 19102. Phone: 215-732-6655. Branch: Newark, New Jersey.

EMPLOYMENT LAW CENTER, Legal Aid Society of San Francisco, 693 Mission Street, 7th floor, San Francisco, California 94105. Phone: 415-495-6420.

ENVIRONMENTAL DEFENSE FUND, 444 Park Avenue South, New York, New York 10016. Phone: 212-686-4191. Branches: Washington, DC; Boulder, Colorado; Berkeley, California, Richmond, Virginia.

EQUAL RIGHTS ADVOCATES, 1370 Mission Street, 4th floor, San Francisco, California 94103. Phone: 415-621-0505.

FLORIDA INSTITUTIONAL LEGAL SERVICES, 2614 South West 34th Street, Gainesville, Florida 32608. Phone: 904-373-3179.

FLORIDA JUSTICE INSTITUTE, INC., 1401 AmeriFirst Building, 1 Southeast Third Avenue, Miami, Florida 33131. Phone: 305-358-2081.

FOOD RESEARCH AND ACTION CENTER (FRAC), 1319 F Street, NW, Suite 500, Washington, DC 20004. Phone: 202-393-5060.

FREEDOM OF INFORMATION CLEARINGHOUSE, 2000 P Street, NW, Suite 700, Washington, DC 20036. Phone: 202-785-3704.

GAY AND LESBIAN ADVOCATES AND DEFENDERS/PARK SQUARE ADVOCATES, INC., 100 Boyleston Street, Suite 900, Boston, Massachusetts 02116. Phone: 617-426-1350.

GOVERNMENT ACCOUNTABILITY PROJECT, 1555 Connecticut Avenue, NW, Washington, DC 20036. Phone: 202-232-8550.

GULF AND GREAT PLAINS LEGAL FOUNDATION, 101 West 11th Street, Kansas City, Missouri 64105. Phone: 816-474-6600. Branch: Houston, Texas.

HARRISON INSTITUTE FOR PUBLIC LAW, Georgetown University Law Center, 605 G Street, NW, Suite 401, Washington, DC 20001. Phone: 202-624-8235.

HOUSING ADVOCATES, INC., 353 Leader Building, Cleveland, Ohio 44114. Phone: 216-579-0575.

IMMIGRATION LAW CLINIC, Columbia University School of Law, 435 West 116th Street, New York, NY 10027. Phone: 212-280-4291.

INDIAN LAW RESOURCE CENTER, 601 E Street, SE, Washington, DC 20003. Phone: 202-547-2800.

INDUSTRIAL COOPERATIVE ASSOCIATION, 249 Elm Street, Somerville, Massachusetts 02144. Phone: 617-628-7330. Branch: Port Washington, New York.

INSTITUTE FOR CHILD ADVOCACY, 2800 Euclid Avenue, Suite 314, Cleveland, Ohio 44115. Phone: 216-579-1460.

INSTITUTE FOR PUBLIC REPRESENTATION, 600 New Jersey Avenue, NW, Washington, DC 20001. Phone: 202-624-8390.

INTERNATIONAL HUMAN RIGHTS LAW GROUP, 1346 Connecticut Avenue, NW, Washington, DC 20036. Phone: 202-659-5023.

JUVENILE JUSTICE LAW CLINIC, Georgetown University Law Center, 605 G Street, NW, (Third floor) Washington, DC 20001. Phone: 202-624-8205.

JUVENILE LAW CENTER, 112 South 16th Street, 7th floor, Philadelphia, Pennsylvania 19102. Phone: 215-563-1933.

LAMBDA LEGAL DEFENSE AND EDUCATION FUND, 132 West 43rd Street, New York, New York 10036. Phone: 212-944-9488.

LAWYERS' COMMITTEE FOR CIVIL RIGHTS UNDER LAW, 1400 I Street, NW, Suite 400, Washington, DC 20005 (National Office). Phone: 202-371-1212. Affiliated Offices: Atlanta, Georgia; Boston, Massachusetts; Chicago, Illinois; Denver, Colorado; San Francisco, Los Angeles, California; Philadelphia, Pennsylvania; Washington, DC (Denver - Colorado Lawyers Committee; Philadelphia - Public Interest Law Center of Philadelphia; Los Angeles - Public Counsel, Boston - LCCRUL of Boston Bar).

LEAGUE OF WOMEN VOTERS EDUCATION FUND/LITIGATION DEPARTMENT, 1730 M Street, NW, Washington, DC 20036. Phone: 202-429-1965.

LEGAL ACTION CENTER, 19 West 44th Street, New York, New York, 10036. Phone: 212-997-0110.

LEGAL COUNSEL FOR THE ELDERLY, 1331 H Street, NW, Washington, DC 20005. Phone: 202-234-0970. Branch: 1909 K Street, NW, Washington, DC 20049.

LEGAL ENVIRONMENTAL ASSISTANCE FOUNDATION, 203 North Gadsden Street, Tallahassee, Florida 32301. Phone: 904-681-2591. Branches: Knoxville, Tennessee; Atlanta, Georgia, Birmingham, Alabama.

LEGAL SERVICES FOR CHILDREN, INC., 149 9th Street, Top Floor, San Francisco, California 94103. Phone: 415-863-3762.

LEGAL SERVICES FOR THE ELDERLY, 132 West 43rd Street, New York, New York 10036. Phone: 212-391-0120.

LESBIAN RIGHTS PROJECT, 1370 Mission Street, 4th floor, San Francisco, California 94103. Phone: 415-621-0674.

MASSACHUSETTS CORRECTIONAL LEGAL SERVICES, 8 Winter Street, 9th floor, Boston, Massachusetts 02108. Phone: 617-482-2773.

MASSACHUSETTS LAW REFORM INSTITUTE, 69 Canal Street, Boston, Massachusetts 02114. Phone: 617-742-9250.

MASSPIRG, 37 Temple Place, Boston, Massachusetts 02111. Phone: 617-423-1796. Branches: Amherst, Worcester, New Bedford, Massachusetts. (Also at 19 college campuses around the state)

MEDIA ACCESS PROJECT, 1609 Connecticut Avenue, NW, Washington, DC 20009. Phone: 202-232-4300.

MENTAL HEALTH ADVOCACY PROJECT, 711 East San Fernando, San Jose, California 95112. Phone: 408-294-9730.

MENTAL HEALTH LAW PROJECT, 2021 L Street, NW, Suite 800, Washington, DC 20036. Phone: 202-467-5730.

MEXICAN AMERICAN LEGAL DEFENSE AND EDUCATION FUND, 28 Geary Street, 6th floor, San Francisco, California 94108. Phone: 415-981-5800. Branches: Washington, DC; Los Angeles, California; Chicago, Illinois; Denver, Colorado; San Antonio, Texas.

MICHIGAN LEGAL SERVICES, 900 Michigan Building, 220 Bagley, Detroit, Michigan 48226. Phone: 313-964-4130. Branch: Lansing, Michigan.

MID-ATLANTIC LEGAL FOUNDATION, 400 Market Street, 3rd floor, Philadelphia, Pennsylvania 19106. Phone: 215-238-1367. Branch: New York, New York.

MIGRANT LEGAL ACTION PROGRAM, 2001 S Street, NW, Washington, DC 20009. Phone: 202-462-7744.

MOUNTAIN STATES LEGAL FOUNDATION, 1200 Lincoln Street, Suite 600, Denver, Colorado 80203. Phone: 303-861-0244.

NAACP LEGAL DEFENSE AND EDUCATIONAL FUND, INC., 99 Hudson Street, 16th floor, New York, New York 10013. Phone: 212-219-1900. Branch: Washington, DC.

NATIONAL ASSOCIATION OF THE DEAF LEGAL DEFENSE FUND, 800 Florida Avenue, NE, P.O. Box 2304, Washington, DC 20002. Phone: 202-651-5461.

NATIONAL CENTER FOR IMMIGRANTS' RIGHTS, 256 South Occidental Boulevard, Los Angeles, California 90057. Phone: 213-388-8693.

NATIONAL CENTER FOR LAW AND THE DEAF, 800 Florida Avenue, NE, Washington, DC 20002. Phone: 202-651-5454. TTY: 202-651-5457.

NATIONAL AUDUBON SOCIETY, 645 Pennsylvania Ave., S.E., Washington, D.C. 20003. Phone: 202-547-9009.

NATIONAL CENTER ON WOMEN AND FAMILY LAW, 799 Broadway, Room 402 New York, New York 10003. Phone: 212-674-8200.

NATIONAL CENTER FOR YOUTH LAW, 1663 Mission Street, 5th floor, San Francisco, California 94103. Phone: 415-543-3307.

NATIONAL COALITION FOR THE HOMELESS, 105 East 22nd Street, New York, New York 10010. Phone: 212-460-8110.

NATIONAL COMMITTEE AGAINST DISCRIMINATION IN HOUSING, 733 15th Street, NW, Suite 1026, Washington, DC 20005. Phone: 202-783-8150.

NATIONAL CONSUMER LAW CENTER, 11 Beacon Street, Room 821, Boston, Massachusetts 02108. Phone: 617-523-8010. Branch: Washington, DC.

NATIONAL ECONOMIC DEVELOPMENT AND LAW CENTER, 1950 Addison Street, Suite 200, Berkeley, California 94704. Phone: 415-548-2600. Branch: Washington, DC.

NATIONAL EMPLOYMENT LAW PROJECT, INC., 475 Riverside Drive, Suite 240, New York, New York 10115. Phone: 212-870-2121. Branch: Washington, DC.

NATIONAL GAY RIGHTS ADVOCATES, 540 Castro Street, San Francisco, California 94114. Phone: 415-863-3624.

NATIONAL HEALTH LAW PROGRAM, 2639 South LaCienega Boulevard, Los Angeles, California 90034. Phone: 213-204-6010. Branch: Washington, DC.

NATIONAL JUVENILE LAW CENTER, 3701 Lindell Boulevard, P.O. Box 14200, St. Louis, Missouri 63178. Phone: 314-652-5555.

NATIONAL ORGANIZATION FOR THE REFORM OF MARIJUANA LAWS (NORML), 2035 P Street, NW, Washington, DC 20036. Phone: 202-331-7363. (Chapters in 40 states).

NATIONAL ORGANIZATION FOR WOMEN LEGAL DEFENSE AND EDUCATION FUND, 99 Hudson Street, New York, New York 10013. Phone: 212-925-6635. Branch: Washington, DC.

NATIONAL PRISON PROJECT OF THE ACLU FOUNDATION, 1346 Connecticut Avenue, NW, Suite 1031, Washington, DC 20036. Phone: 202-331-0500.

NATIONAL SENIOR CITIZENS LAW CENTER, 1302 18th Street, NW, Suite 701, Washington, DC 20036. Phone: 202-887-5280.

NATIONAL WILDLIFE FEDERATION, 1412 16th Street, NW, Washington, DC 20036 (Resources Defense Division). Phone: 202-797-6800. Resource Centers: Boulder, Colorado; Eugene, Oregon; Anchorage Alaska; Missoula, Montana.

NATIONAL WOMEN'S LAW CENTER, 1751 N Street, NW, Washington, DC 20036. Phone: 202-872-0670.

NATIONAL WOMEN'S LAW FUND, SUITE 400, 1101 Euclid Street, Cleveland, Ohio 44115. Phone: 216-621-3443.

NATIVE AMERICAN RIGHTS FUND, 1506 Broadway, Boulder, Colorado 80302. Phone: 303-447-8760. Branch: Washington, DC.

NATURAL RESOURCES DEFENSE COUNCIL, 122 East 42nd Street, New York, New York 10017. Phone: 212-949-0049. Affiliated offices: Washington, DC; San Francisco, California; Denver, Colorado.

NEW ENGLAND LEGAL FOUNDATION, 55 Union Street, Boston, Massachusetts 02108. Phone: 617-367-0174.

NEW YORK LAWYERS FOR THE PUBLIC INTEREST, INC., 36 West 44th Street, Suite 1316, New York, New York 10036. Phone: 212-575-5138.

NORTHWEST ENVIRONMENTAL DEFENSE CENTER, 10015 Southwest Terwilliger Boulevard, Portland, Oregon 97219. Phone: 503-244-1181, ext. 707.

NORTHWEST LABOR AND EMPLOYMENT LAW OFFICE, 705 Second Avenue, Seattle, Washington 98104. Phone: 206-623-1590.

NORTHWEST WOMEN'S LAW CENTER, 119 South Main Street, Suite 330, Seattle, Washington 98104. Phone: 206-682-9552.

OFICINA LEGAL DEL PUEBLO UNIDO, P.O. Box 1493, San Juan, Texas 78589. Phone: 512-787-8171.

1000 FRIENDS OF OREGON, 519 Southwest Third, Room 400, Portland, Oregon 97204. Phone: 503-2230-4396.

PACIFIC LEGAL FOUNDATION, 455 Capitol Mall, Suite 465, Sacramento, California 95814. Phone: 916-444-0154.

PACIFIC NORTHWEST RESOURCES CLINIC, University of Oregon School of Law, Eugene, Oregon 97403. Phone: 503-681-3823.

PRISON LAW CLINIC, Rutgers University School of Law, 15 Washington Street, Newark, New Jersey 07102. Phone: 201-648-5978.

PROJECT JUSTICE AND EQUALITY, 475 Broadway, Gary, Indiana 46402. Phone: 219-883-0384. Branch: Valparaiso, Indiana.

PUBLIC ADVOCATES, INC., 1535 Mission Street, San Francisco, California 94103 Phone: 415-431-7430.

PUBLIC CITIZEN LITIGATION GROUP, 2000 P Street, NW, Suite 700, Washington, DC 20036. Phone: 202-785-3704.

PUBLIC COUNSEL, 3535 West 6th Street, Suite 100, Los Angeles, California 90020. Phone: 213-385-2977.

PUBLIC EDUCATION ASSOCIATION, Litigation Department, 20 West 40th Street, New York, New York 10018. Phone: 212-354-6100.

PUBLIC INTEREST LAW CENTER OF PHILADELPHIA, 1315 Walnut Street, Suite 1600, Philadelphia, Pennsylvania 19107. Phone: 215-735-7200.

PUBLIC INTEREST LAW CLINIC, Practicing Law Center, American University School of Law, 4400 Massachusetts Avenue, NW, Washington, DC 20016. Phone: 202-686-2629. (formerly associated with the National Veterans Law Center, now see Vietnam Veterans of America Legal Services)

REPORTERS' COMMITTEE FOR FREEDOM OF THE PRESS, 800 18th Street, NW, Suite 300, Washington, DC 20006. Phone: 202-466-6313.

REPORTERS'S COMMITTEE FOR FREEDOM OF THE PRESS, 800 18th Street, NW, Suite 300, Washington, DC 20006. Phone: 202-466-6313.

REPRODUCTIVE FREEDOM PROJECT of the ACLU, 132 West 43rd Street, New York, New York 10017. Phone: 212-944-9800.

ROGER BALDWIN FOUNDATION OF THE ACLU, 220 South State Street, Suite 816, Chicago, Illinois 60604. Phone: 312-427-7330.

SAN FRANCISCO LAWYERS' COMMITTEE FOR URBAN AFFAIRS, 625 Market Street, Suite 915, San Francisco, California 94105. Phone: 415-543-9444.

SANTA CLARA COUNTY BAR ASSOCIATION LAW FOUNDATION, INC., 111 North Market Street, Suite 712, San Jose, California 95115. Phone: 408-294-9730. (Affiliated with Mental Health Advocacy Project and Public Interest Law Firm, San Jose)

SIERRA CLUB LEGAL DEFENSE FUND, 2044 Fillmore Street, San Francisco, California 94115. Phone: 415-567-6100. Branches: Denver, Colorado; Juneau, Alaska; Washington, DC.

SOUTHEASTERN LEGAL FOUNDATION, INC., 2900 Chamblee-Tucker Road, Building 4, Atlanta, Georgia, 30341. Phone: 404-458-8313.

SOUTHERN LEGAL COUNSEL, INC., 115 North East 7th Avenue, Suite A, Gainesville, Florida 32601. Phone: 904-377-8288.

SOUTHERN POVERTY LAW CENTER, 1001 South Hull Street, Montgomery, Alabama 36104. Phone: 205-264-0286.

SOUTHERN PRISONERS DEFENSE COMMITTEE, 600 Healy Building, 57 Forsyth Street, Atlanta, Georgia 30303. Phone: 404-688-1202.

TRIAL LAWYERS FOR PUBLIC JUSTICE, P.C., 2000 P Street, NW, Washington, DC 20036. Phone: 202-463-8600.

TRUSTEES FOR ALASKA, INC., 833 Gambell Street, Suite B, Anchorage, Alaska 99501. Phone: 907-276-4244.

UCLA COMMUNICATIONS LAW PROGRAM, School of Law, University of California at Los Angeles, Los Angeles, California 90024. Phone: 213-825-6211.

UNTAPPED RESOURCES, INC., 60 First Avenue, New York, New York 10009. Phone: 212-532-4422. (c/o Brewer)

URBAN LEGAL CLINIC, Rutgers University School of Law, 15 Washington Street, Newark, New Jersey 07102. Phone: 201-648-5576.

VIETNAM VETERANS OF AMERICA LEGAL SERVICES, 2001 S Street, NW, Suite 702, Washington, DC 20009. Phone: 202-686-2599 *or* 202-322-2700. (Formerly the National Veterans Law Center)

WASHINGTON LAWYERS' COMMITTEE FOR CIVIL RIGHTS UNDER LAW, 1400 I Street, NW, Suite 450, Washington, DC 20005. Phone: 202-371-1212.

WESTERN CENTER ON LAW AND POVERTY, INC., 3535 West Sixth Street, Los Angeles, California 90020. Phone: 213-487-7211.

WESTERN LAW CENTER FOR THE HANDICAPPED at Loyola Law School, 1441 West Olympic Boulevard, P.O. Box 15019, Los Angeles, California 90015. Phone: 213-736-1031.

WOMEN'S LAW PROJECT, 112 South 16th Street, Suite 1012, Philadelphia, Pennsylvania 19102. Phone: 215-564-6280.

WOMEN'S LEGAL DEFENSE FUND, 2000 P Street, NW, Suite 400, Washington, DC 20036. Phone: 202-887-0364.

WOMEN'S RIGHTS LITIGATION CLINIC, Rutgers University School of Law, 15 Washington Street, Newark, New Jersey 07102. Phone: 201-648-5637.

WOMEN'S RIGHTS PROJECT OF THE ACLU, 132 West 43rd Street, New York, New York 10036. Phone: 212-944-9800. Branch: Richmond, Virginia.

YOUTH POLICY AND LAW CENTER, 30 West Mifflin, Room 904, Madison, Wisconsin 53703. Phone: 608-263-5533. Branch: Milwaukee, Wisconsin.

PRIMARY PROGRAM EMPHASIS

CLIENT-DEFINED CENTERS

Children

Advocates for Children of New York
Children's Defense Fund
Children's Rights Group
Children's Rights Project - ACLU
Education Law Center
Institute for Child Advocacy
Juvenile Justice Law Clinic (Georgetown University)
Legal Services for Children
Juvenile Law Center of Philadelphia
National Center for Youth Law - (LSC)
National Juvenile Law Center
Public Education Association (Litigation Department)
Youth Policy and Law Center

Disabled*

Advocacy Center for the Elderly and Disabled
Advocacy, Inc.
American Council of the Blind
Bay Area Center for Law and the Deaf
Carolina Legal Assistance for Mental Health
Center for Law and Health Science
Community Health Law Project
Disability Rights Center
Disability Rights Education Defense Fund
Mental Health Advocacy Project
Mental Health Law Project
Mental Association of the Deaf Legal Defense Fund
National Center for Law and the Deaf
Santa Clara County Bar Association Law Foundation
Untapped Resources, Inc.
Western Law Center for the Handicapped

Elderly

Legal Counsel for the Elderly
Legal Services for the Elderly
National Senior Citizens Law Center

---

*Each state also has a federally-funded program designed to protect the rights of the developmentally disabled. A directory of state programs can be obtained from the Administration on Developmental Disabilities, Dept. of Health and Human Services, Room 343E, 200 Indiana Avenue, SW, Washington, D.C., 20201, or by calling 202-245-2897.

Gay/Lesbian

American Association for Personal Property
Gay and Lesbian Advocates and Defenders
Lambda Legal Defense and Education Fund
Lesbian Rights Project
National Gay Rights Advocates

Women

Connecticut Women's Educational and Legal Fund, Inc.
Equal Rights Advocates
National Center on Women and Family Law (LSC)
NOW Legal Defense and Education Fund
National Women's Law Center
National Women's Law Fund
Northwest Women's Law Center
Reproductive Freedom Project - ACLU
Women's Law Project
Women's Legal Defense Fund
Women's Rights Litigation Clinic
Women's Rights Project - ACLU

Minorities - Other

Asian American Legal Defense and Education Fund
Asian Law Caucus
Chicano Education Project
Indian Law Resource Center
Mexican American Legal Defense and Education Fund
NAACP Legal Defense and Educational Fund, Inc.
Native American Rights Fund
Oficina Legal del Pueblo Unido
Puerto Rican Legal Defense and Education Fund
Vietnam Veterans of America Legal Services

CAUSE-DEFINED CENTERS

Civil Rights/Civil Liberties

American Civil Liberties Union/ACLU Foundation
ACLU Project on National Security and Civil Liberties
Chicago Lawyers' Committee for Civil Rights Under Law
Florida Justice Institute
Lawyers' Committee for Civil Rights Under Law
Lawyers' Committee for Civil Rights Under Law of the Boston Bar Association
League of Women Voters Education Fund - Litigation Dept.
National Committee Against Discrimination in Housing
Roger Baldwin Foundation of the ACLU
Washington Lawyers' Committee for Civil Rights Under Law

Communications/Media

Citizens Communication Center
Communications Media Center
Media Access Project
Reporters' Committee for Freedom of the Press
UCLA Communications Law Program

Consumers

Aviation Consumer Action Project
Center for Applied Legal Studies
Center for Auto Safety
Consumers Union/Litigation Office
Center for Science in the Public Interest

Employment

Employment Law Center of the Legal Aid Society of San Francisco (also Poverty)
Industrial Cooperative Association, Legal Support Project
Migrant Legal Action Program (also Poverty)
National Employment Law Project (LSC)
Northwest Labor and Employment Law Office

Environment

Connecticut Fund for the Environment
Conservation Law Foundation of New England
Environmental Defense Fund
Legal Environmental Assistance Foundation
National Wildlife Federation - Resources Defense Division
Natural Resources Defense Council
Northwest Environmental Defense Center
1000 Friends of Oregon
Pacific Northwest Resource Clinic
Sierra Club Legal Defense Fund
Trustees for Alaska

Immigration and International

Alien Rights Law Project (see Washington LCCRUL)
Immigration Law Clinic
International Human Rights Law Group
National Center for Immigration Rights

Housing

Housing Advocates

National Coalition for the Homeless
National Committee Against Discrimination in Housing (also Civil Rights)

Multi-Issue

Arizona Center for Law in the Public Interest
Business and Professional People for the Public Interest
Center for Constitutional Rights
Center for Governmental Responsibility
Center for Law and Social Policy
Center for Law in the Public Interest
Center for Public Representation
Constitutional Litigation Clinic
Government Accountability Project
Harrison Institute for Public Law
Institute for Public Representation
MASS PIRG
Public Citizen Litigation Group
Public Interest Law Center of Philadelphia
Public Interest Law Clinic
San Francisco Lawyers' Committee
Southern Legal Counsel

Poverty

Advocates for Basic Legal Equality
Appalachian Research and Defense Fund
Center for Social Welfare Policy and Law (LSC)
Colorado Coalition of Legal Services Programs
Colorado Lawyers' Committee
Employment Law Center (see Employment)
Food Research and Action Center
Massachusetts Law Reform Institute
Michigan Legal Services
Migrant Legal Action Program (see Employment)
National Economic Development and Law Center (LSC)
National Health Law Project (LSC)
Project Justice and Equality
Public Advocates
Southern Poverty Law Center
Urban Legal Clinic
Western Center on Law and Poverty

Prisoners/Ex-Offenders

Florida Institutional Legal Services
Legal Action Center
Massachusetts Correctional Legal Services

112

National Prison Project - ACLU
Prison Law Clinic
Southern Prisoners' Defense Committee

Business-Oriented/Free Enterprise

Capital Legal Foundation
Gulf and Great Plains Legal Foundation
Mid-Atlantic Legal Foundation
Mountain States Legal Foundation
New England Legal Foundation
Southeastern Legal Foundation
Pacific Legal Foundation

Other

Center for Rural Affairs
Freedom of Information Clearinghouse
National Organization for the Reform of Marijuana Laws
Public Counsel

Legal Services Corporation National Support Projects

Center for Law and Education (see Children)
Center on Social Welfare Policy and Law (see Poverty)
Indian Law Resource Center (see Other Minorities)
Migrant Legal Action Project (see Employment)
National Center for Immigrants' Rights (see Immigration)
National Center on Women and Family Law (see Women)
National Center for Youth Law (see Children)
National Consumer Law Center (see Consumers)
National Economic Development and Law Center (see Poverty)
National Employment Law Project (see Employment)
National Health Law Program (see Poverty)
National Senior Citizens Law Center (see Elderly)

(The primary function of national support projects is to assist local Legal
Services programs in specialized areas of the law.)

LOCATION OF MAIN OFFICE

ALABAMA
Southern Poverty Law Center, Montgomery
ALASKA
Trustees for Alaska, Anchorage
ARIZONA
Arizona Center for Law in the Public Interest, Phoenix
CALIFORNIA
    American Association for Personal Privacy, San Francisco
    Asian Law Caucus, Oakland
    Bay Area Center for Law and the Deaf, San Leandro
    Center for Law in the Public Interest, Los Angeles
    Children's Rights Group, San Francisco
    Disability Rights Education Defense Fund, Inc., Berkeley
    Employment Law Center, San Francisco
    Equal Rights Advocates, San Francisco
    Lesbian Rights Project, San Francisco
    Legal Services for Children, Inc., San Francisco
    Mental Health Advocacy Project, San Jose
    Mexican American Legal Defense and Education Fund, San Francisco
    National Center for Immigrants' Rights, Los Angeles
    National Center for Youth Law, San Francisco
    National Economic Development and Law Project, Berkeley
    National Gay Rights Advocates, San Francisco
    National Health Law Program, Los Angeles
    Pacific Legal Foundation, Sacramento
    Public Counsel, Los Angeles
    San Francisco Lawyers' Committee for Urban Affairs, San Francisco
    Santa Clara County Bar Association Law Foundation, San Jose
    Sierra Club Legal Defense Fund, San Francisco
    UCLA Communications Law Program, Los Angeles
    Western Center on Law and Poverty, Los Angeles
    Western Law Center for the Handicapped, Los Angeles

COLORADO
    Chicano Education Project, Denver
    Colorado Coalition of Legal Services Programs, Denver
    Colorado Lawyers' Committee, Denver
    Mountain States Legal Foundation, Denver
    Native American Rights Fund, Boulder

CONNECTICUT
    Connecticut Fund for the Environment, New Haven
    Connecticut Women's Educational and Legal Fund, Hartford

DISTRICT OF COLUMBIA
  ACLU Project on National Security and Civil Liberties
  American Council of the Blind
  Aviation Consumer Action Project
  Capital Legal Foundation
  Center for Applied Legal Studies
  Center for Auto Safety
  Center for Law and Social Policy
  Center for Science in the Public Interest
  Children's Defense Fund
  Citizens Communication Center
  Consumers Union, Litigation Office
  Disability Rights Center
  Food Research and Action Center
  Freedom of Information Clearinghouse
  Government of Accountability Project
  Harrison Institute for Public Law
  Indian Law Resource Center
  Institute for Public Representation
  International Human Rights Law Group
  Juvenile Justice Law Clinic
  Lawyers Committee for Civil Rights Under Law
  League of Women Voters Education Fund, Litigation Dept.
  Legal Counsel for the Elderly
  Media Access Project
  Mental Health Law Project
  Migrant Legal Action Project
  National Association of the Deaf Legal Defense Fund
  National Center for Law and the Deaf
  National Committee Against Discrimination in Housing
  National Organization for the Reform of Marijuana Laws
  National Prison Project of the ACLU Foundation
  National Senior Citizens Law Center
  National Wildlife Federation, Resources Defense Division
  National Women's Law Center
  Public Citizen Litigation Group
  Public Interest Law Clinic
  Reporters' Committee for Freedom of the Press
  Trial Lawyers for Public Justice
  Vietnam Veterans of America Legal Services
  Washington Lawyers' Committee for Civil Rights Under Law
  Women's Legal Defense Fund
FLORIDA
  Florida Institutional Legal Services, Gainesville
  Florida Justice Institute, Inc., Miami
  Legal Environmental Assistance Foundation, Tallahassee
  Southern Legal Counsel, Inc., Gainesville

116

GEORGIA
Southeastern Legal Foundation, Inc., Atlanta
Southern Prisoners Defense Committee, Atlanta
ILLINOIS
Business and Professional People for the Public Interest, Chicago
Chicago Lawyers' Committee for Civil Rights Under Law, Chicago
Roger Baldwin Foundation of the ACLU, Chicago
INDIANA
Project Justice and Equality, Gary
LOUISIANA
Advocacy Center for the Elderly and Disabled, New Orleans
MASSACHUSETTS
Center for Law and Education, Cambridge
Conservation Law Foundation of New England, Boston
Center on Law and Health Science, Boston
Gay and Lesbian Advocates and Defenders, Boston
Industrial Cooperative Association, Somerville
Massachusetts Correctional Legal Services, Inc., Boston
Massachusetts Law Reform Institute, Boston
MASS PIRG (Public Interest Research Group), Boston
National Consumer Law Center, Boston
New England Legal Foundation, Boston
MICHIGAN
Michigan Legal Services, Detroit
MISSOURI
Gulf and Great Plains Legal Foundation, Kansas City
National Juvenile Law Center, St. Louis
NEBRASKA
Center for Rural Affairs, Walthill
NEW JERSEY
Community Health Law Project, East Orange
Constitutional Litigation Clinic, Newark
Prison Law Clinic, Newark
Urban Legal Clinic, Newark
Women's Rights Litigation Clinic, Newark
NEW YORK
Advocates for Children of New York, Long Island City
ACLU/ACLU Foundation, NYC
Asian American Legal Defense and Education Fund, NYC
Center for Constitutional Rights, NYC
Center on Social Welfare Policy and Law, NYC
Children's Rights Project/ACLU, NYC
Communications Media Center, NYC
Community Development Legal Assistance Center, NYC
Environmental Defense Fund, NYC
Immigration Law Clinic, NYC
Lambda Legal Defense and Education Fund, NYC

Legal Action Center, NYC
Legal Services for the Elderly, NYC
NAACP Legal Defense and Educational Fund, Inc., NYC
National Center on Women and Family Law, NYC
National Coalition for the Homeless, NYC
National Employment Law Project, NYC
NOW Legal Defense and Education Fund, NYC
Natural Resources Defense Council, NYC
New York Lawyers for the Public Interest, NYC
Public Education Association, Litigation Department, NYC
Puerto Rican Legal Defense Fund, Inc., NYC
Reproductive Freedom Project/ACLU, NYC
Untapped Resources, Inc., NYC
Women's Rights Project/ACLU, NYC

NORTH CAROLINA
Carolina Legal Assistance, Mental Disability Law Project, Raleigh

OHIO
Advocates for Basic Legal Equality, Toledo
Housing Advocates, Inc., Cleveland
Institute for Child Advocacy, Cleveland
National Women's Law Fund, Cleveland

OREGON
Northwest Environmental Defense Center, Portland
1000 Friends of Oregon, Portland
Pacific Northwest Resource Clinic, Eugene

PENNSYLVANIA
Education Law Center, Philadelphia
Juvenile Law Center of Philadelphia
Mid-Atlantic Legal Foundation, Philadelphia
Public Interest Law Center of Philadelphia
Women's Law Project, Philadelphia

TEXAS
Advocacy, Inc., Austin
Oficina Legal del Pueblo, San Juan

WASHINGTON
Northwest Labor and Employment Law Office, Seattle
Northwest Women's Law Center, Seattle

WEST VIRGINIA
Appalachian Research and Defense Fund, Charleston

WISCONSIN
Center for Public Representation, Madison
Youth Policy and Law Center, Madison

Appendix II
LSC NATIONAL SUPPORT CENTERS

The Legal Services Corporation funds 17 national support centers to provide specialized expertise to local legal services programs. While national support center services are available through local legal services programs, the centers are also willing to provide services directly to PBI programs. Although services vary by center, they generally can provide assistance in: training in their subject areas, resource materials in their subject areas, and case assistance. A packet describing in more detail resources from all centers is available from National Economic Development and Law Center, 1950 Addison St., Berkeley, CA, 94704, (415) 548-2600, or contact the program directly.

Center for Law and Education
Larson Hall, 6th floor
6 Appian Way
Cambridge, MA 02138
(617) 495-4666
Contact: Paul Newman
School-related problems including special education needs of handicapped children, student discipline, bilingual/bicultural education, discriminatory school policies, testing and tracking, federal programs, and parent/student/community participation.

119

Center on Social Welfare Policy and Law
95 Madison Ave., Room 701
New York, NY 10016
(212) 679-3709
Contact: Henry Freedman
Cash welfare programs, particularly Aid to
Families With Dependent Children (AFDC),
Supplemental Security Income (SSI), and state and
local General Assistance programs.

Food Research and Action Center (FRAC)
1319 F St., N.W.
Washington, D.C. 20004
(202) 393-5060
Contact: Michael R. Lemov
Federal food programs including food stamps,
school lunch and breakfast, elderly nutrition,
child care food, summer food, and Women, Infants
and Children (WIC) programs.

Indian Law Support Center
Native American Rights Fund
1506 Broadway
Boulder, CO 80302
(303) 447-8760
Contact: Steven Moore
Preservation of tribal existence, protection of tribal
resources, promotion of human rights,
accountability of governments, and development of
Indian law.

Mental Health Law Project
2021 "L" St.
Washington, DC 20036
(202) 467-5730
Contact: Norman Rosenberg

Representation of mentally disabled persons.

Migrant Legal Action Program
2001 S St., N.W., #310
Washington, D.C. 20009
(202) 462-7744
Contact: Executive Director
Issues affecting migrant and seasonal farmworkers,
especially concerning the Migrant and Seasonal
Agricultural Worker Protection Act (AWPA), Fair
Labor Standards Act (FLSA), Foreign Workers
("H-2" Program), pesticides, migrant education,
and migrant housing.

National Center for Immigrants Rights
1636 W. 8th St., #215
Los Angeles, CA 90017
(213) 487-2531
Contact: Charles Wheeler
Immigration and alien's rights matters.

National Center on Women and Family Law
799 Broadway, Room 402
New York, NY 10003
(212) 674-8200
Contact: Laurie Woods
Women's issues in family law, especially child custody,
child support enforcement, and battered women.

National Center for Youth Law
1663 Mission St., 5th Flr.
San Francisco, CA 94103
(415) 543-3307
Contact: Alice Bussiere
Juvenile courts; the problems of children and
adolescents who live in institutions; abuse, neglect,

and termination proceedings; foster care; youth employment; special problems of adolescent health; housing discrimination against families with children; child nutrition; and governmental benefit programs specifically directed at poor children.

National Consumer Law Center
11 Beacon St., #821
Boston, MA 02108
(617) 523-8010
Contact: Robert Sable
Consumer issues, including bankruptcies, deceptive sales practices, purchases of shoddy or defective goods or services, odometer tampering, debt collection harassment, repossessions, misleading credit terms, credit discrimination, credit overcharges and faulty credit reports. Energy issues including utility shutoffs, deposit requirements, rights to fuel assistance, and other energy assistance programs.

National Economic Development and Law Project
1950 Addison St.
Berkeley, CA 94704
(415) 548-2600
Contact: David Kirkpatrick

Assists eligible client groups in developing housing, jobs, and needed services in low-income communities; deals with legal issues surrounding development of health services and health ventures; helps establish small business investment corporations and other financial institutions serving the low-income community; interprets the rights of community groups under federal grants;

advises community groups on the use of block grants for community-based economic development; and structures community-based non-profit activities in conjunction with the private sector.

National Employment Law Project
475 Riverside Dr., Suite 240
New York, NY 10027
(212) 870-2121
Contact: Barbara Morris
Employment law including wrongful discharges, unemployment compensation, federal training and jobs programs, employment discrimination, public employment rights, employment rights of the handicapped, minimum wage and health and safety laws, employee benefits and union related issues.

National Health Law Program
2639 S. La Cienege Blvd.
Los Angeles, CA 90034
(213) 204-6010
Contact: Sylvia Drew Ivie
Health law issues affecting the poor including Medicaid, Medicare, cost containment, Hill-Burton Act, civil rights, maternal and child health, and state and local responsibility to provide indigent health care.

National Housing & Community Development Law Project
1950 Addison St.
Berkeley, CA 94704
(415) 548-9400
Contact: David Madway
Private landlord/tenant law, community

development, housing development and preservation, displacement and relocation, public housing and Section 8 issues, rural housing, HUD subsidized multifamily housing, and federally-financed single family housing.

National Senior Citizens Law Center
2025 M St. N.W. #400
Washington, D.C. 20036
(202) 887-5280
Contact: Burton Fretz
Legal problems of the elderly including Social Security retirement and survivors' benefits, Supplemental Security Income disability benefits, Medicare, nursing homes and long-term care problems, private pensions, public pensions, age discrimination, mandatory retirement, and services available under the Older Americans Act and Title XX of the Social Security Act.

National Social Science and Law Center
1990 M Street, N.W., Suite 700
Washington, D.C. 20036
(202) 797-1100
Contact: Leonard H. Goodman
Application of quantitative methods to legal issues; processing and analysis of data for use in argument; class estimates; survey design; graphic presentation of demographic and economic data.

National Veterans Legal Services Project, Inc.
2001 S. St., N.W., #702
Washington, D.C. 20009
(202) 686- 2741
Contact: Bart Stichman
Veterans' law issues including discharge upgrading.

Appendix III
TECHNICAL RESOURCES AVAILABLE TO ASSIST IN PUBLIC INTEREST CASES
Computer Assisted Legal Research Services

The Legal Services Corporation supports six regional computer-assisted legal research (CALR) projects throughout the country to provide LEXIS, WESTLAW and other data base research to legal services programs. Depending upon arrangements with local legal services programs, CALR can be offered for cases taken through a private bar involvement project. An information packet can be obtained from National Clearinghouse for Legal Services, 407 S. Dearborn, Suite 400, Chicago, IL 60605, (312) 939-3830, or contact the programs listed below.

Massachusetts Law Reform
69 Canal St., 2nd Flr.
Boston, MA 02114
(800) 225-2044 (outside MASS)
(617) 742-9335 or 9334 (in MASS)
Serves Connecticut, Maine, Vermont, Massachusetts, New Hampshire, Rhode Island Idaho and Montana.

Greater Upstate Law Project
101 Powers Bldg.
16 W. Main St.
Rochester, NY 14614
(716) 454-6500

Serves New York State.

Ohio State Legal Services
155 N. High St.
Columbus, OH 43215
(800) 848-0180 (outside OH) or
   (800) 282-2769 (in OH)
Serves Delaware, Washington, D.C., Maryland,
Michigan, New Jersey, Ohio, Pennsylvania and
West Virginia, and Alaska.

National Clearinghouse for Legal Services
407 S. Dearborn St., #400
Chicago, IL 60605
(800) 621-3256 (outside IL) or (312) 939-3834 (in IL)
Serves Arizona, Colorado, Illinois, Indiana, Iowa,
Kansas, Minnesota, Missouri, Nebraska, New
Mexico, North Dakota, Oklahoma, Texas, Utah,
Wisconsin and Indian Law Projects, Hawaii, Guam,
Micronesia and Oregon.

Legal Aid Society of Northwest North Carolina
216 W. 4th St., Patten Bldg.
Winston-Salem, NC 27101
(919) 725-9166
Serves Alabama, Arkansas, Florida, Georgia,
Kentucky, Louisiana, Mississippi, North Carolina
and Tennessee, Washington, and Wyoming.

Western Center on Law & Poverty
3535 W. 6th St.
Los Angeles, CA 90020
(213) 487-7211

Serves California and Nevada.

Finances

Accounting Services

Accountants for the Public Interest
888 17th St., N.W.
Suite 201
Washington, D.C. 20006
(202) 659-3797
Contact: Peter D. Rosenstein, Executive Director

API, a national non-profit organization headquartered in Washington, D.C., encourages accountants to volunteer their services in their communities. API affiliates, located in Chicago, Newark, New York City, Philadelphia, Portland, Providence, Oklahoma City, and Los Angeles, provide technical assistance to non-profit organizations, small businesses, and low-income people who cannot afford to purchase needed accounting services. In areas where an affiliate is not located, the national headquarters will attempt to identify accountants who are interested in public service work. API also provides objective, independent analysis of the accounting dimensions of local public policy issues.

Fundraising

Grantsmanship Center
1031 S. Grand Ave.
Los Angeles, CA 90015-1492
(800) 421-9512

A for-profit organization designed to provide how-to-skills for the grant application process. Conducts workshops throughout the nation. A free catalog of publications and services is available.

The Foundation Center
888 Seventh Ave.
New York, NY 10106
(212) 975-1120

The Foundation Center is an independent national service organization established by foundations to provide an authoritative source of information on philanthropic giving. The Center gathers and disseminates information on private giving through its libraries, public service programs, and publications. The Center prepares and publishes directories, indexes, and technical assistance materials which provide detailed information on philanthropic resources. It maintains for free public use a national network of library collections offering reference and educational services, as well as a comprehensive collection of foundation and corporate giving materials. To check on locations call toll-free (800) 424-9836.

IOLTA Information

National IOLTA Clearinghouse
Florida Justice Institute, Inc.
1401 AmeriFirst Bldg.
One S.E. Third Ave.
Miami, FL 33131
(305) 358-2081
Contact: Randall Berg, Executive Director

IOLTA programs have been approved in thirty-eight states and the District of Columbia, as of December 1985. The National IOLTA (Interest on Lawyers' Trust Accounts) Clearinghouse provides information, materials, training, and technical assistance on IOLTA program design and operation. The Clearinghouse is co-sponsored by a nationally representative advisory committee; the ABA is one of the Clearinghouse's co-sponsoring organizations.

National Legal Associations

Corporate Counsel Organizations

Pro Bono Program of the American Corporate
  Counsel Institute
1225 Connecticut Ave., Suite 202
Washington, D.C. 20036
(202) 296-4523
Contact: Timothy Winslow, Staff Director
Works to mobilize and to provide educational, technical, and networking assistance for corporate pro bono services nationwide; works to develop corporate pro bono programs as well as pro bono work by individual attorneys; conducts regional seminars and continuing seminar follow-up activities; seeks to institute pro bono committees and programs within local ACCA chapters; produces publications and videotapes on administrative and substantive aspects of corporate pro bono activities; refines existing corporate pro bono program models and develops new models; generates statistics on corporate pro bono programs and maintains a pro bono information and networking center for ACCA members and other interested parties.

Legal Professional Organizations
The following are national headquarters for various legal professional organizations. Although the national organizations may not have a formal statement regarding participation in pro bono

activities, individuals in local affiliates may be
willing to participate. Please contact the national
headquarters for information on local affiliates.

National Association of Legal Assistants
1420 S. Utica
Tulsa, OK 74104
(918) 587-6828
Contact: Marge Dover, Executive Director

National Federation of Paralegal Associations
P. O. Box 40158
Overland Park, KS 66204
(913) 381-4458
Contact: Sandra L. Sabanske, Executive Director

National Association of Legal Secretaries
2250 East 73rd Street, Suite 550
Tulsa, OK 74136
(918) 493-3540
Contact: Judy Kruse, Executive Administrator

National Shorthand Reporters Association
118 Park St., S.E.
Vienna, VA 22180
(703) 281-4677
Contact: Marshall Jorpeland, Communication Director
For more details: Michael Conway Pro Bono
Activator of the ABA PBI Project. (312) 988-5771

Newly-initiated program designed to recruit
shorthand reporters to provide reporting services
to recognized local servcies and bar association
pro bono programs.

BIBLIOGRAPHY

Agnew, "What's Wrong with the Legal Services Program," 58 A.B.A.J. 930 (1972)

Alliance for Justice, "Summary of Results—Survey of Public Interest Law Centers" (unpublished, 1985)

American Bar Association, "Goals" (1986)

American Bar Association, "ABA Litigation Section: Pro Bono Recruitment Project" (1985)

American Bar Association, *Annotated Model Rules of Professional Conduct* (1984)

Arriola & Wolinsky, "Public Interest Practice in Practice: The Law in Reality," 34 Hastings L. J. 1207 (1983)

Auerbach, *Unequal Justice: Lawyers and Social Change in Modern America* (1976)

Baer, "From Nader's Raiders to Morrison's Militia," 9 *Legal Times* 1 (July 14, 1986)

Becker, "In Defense of an Embattled Mode of Advocacy: An Analysis and Justification of Public Interest Practice," 90 Yale L. J. 1436 (1981)

Bellows and Kettleson, "From Ethics to Politics: Confronting Scarcity and Fairness in Public Interest Practice," 58 B.U.L. Rev. 336 (1978)

Belton, "Some Thoughts on the 'New' Law School Constitutency: The Public Interest Lawyer," 35 Mercer L. Rev. 859 (1984)

Berlin, Roisman and Kessler, "Public Interest Law," 38 Geo. Wash. L. Rev. 675 (1970)

Blodgett, "Secular Values?: Parents Sue Over School Texts," 72 A.B.A.J. 27 (1986)

Bloustein, "Social Responsibility, Public Policy & the Law Schools," 55 N.Y.U. L. Rev. 207 (1976)

Breger, "Accountability and the Adjudication of the Public Interest," 8 Harv. J. L. & Pub. Pol'y (1985)

Cahn and Cahn, "Power to the People or the Profession—the Public Interest in Public Interest Law," 79 Yale L. J. 1005 (1970)

Carlin, Howard & Messinger, *Civil Justice and the Poor* (1966)

Castro, *Chicago Power* (1974)

Christianson, *Lawyers for People of Moderate Means* (1970)

Clark, "After a Decade of Doing Battle, Public Interest Groups Show their Age," 28 Nat'l J. 1136 (July 12, 1980)

Congress Watch, "The Power of Pacs," (November 1981)

Cook, "Picket Limit Angers Pro-lifers," 8 Nat'l L. J. 3 (July 14, 1986)

Council for Public Interest Law, *Balancing the Scales of Justice* (1976)

Dombroff, "Members of the Service Suing the U.S.: Is the Feres Doctrine Crumbling?," 8 Nat'l L. J. 16 (March 10, 1986)

Eagleton, "Rights Without Remedies: The Burger Court in Full Bloom," 63 Wash. U. L. Q. 351 (1986)

Edwards, "The Ethical Dilemma: Serving the Public Interest or Personal Interest," 7 Wash. U. L. Sch. Mag. 8 (1985)

Effron, "He's Not Humble—But He Gets Results," 8 Nat'l L. J. 1 (March 10, 1986)

Eisenberg, "Ordinary and Extra-Ordinary Institutional Litigation," 93 Harv. L. Rev. 465 (1980)

Ellis, *Taking Ideals Seriously: The Case for a Lawyer's Public Interest Movement* (1984)

Ely, "Business Law Versus Public Interest Law: A False Dichotomy," 18 Stan. L. Rev. (Fall 1983)

Fadil, "Citizen Suits Against Polluters: Picking up the Pace," 9 Harv. Envir. L. Rev. 23 (1985)

Fess, "Forms of Justice," 93 Harv. L. Rev. 1 (1979)

First, "Competition in the Legal Education Industry," 53 N.Y.U. L. Rev. 311 (1978)

Ford Foundation, *1985 Annual Report*

Ford Foundation and A.B.A. Public Interest Practice Committee, *Public Interest Law: Five Years Later (1976)*

Foundation Center, *The Foundation Directory* (1986)

Geoghegan, "The Angst of an Aging Activist: Warren Court Children," *The New Republic* at 17 (May 19, 1986)

Gepp, "New Tactics in Civil Rights Actions," 6 Cal. Lawyer 49 (April 1986)

Greenberg, "Litigation for Social Change: Methods, Limits and Role in Democracy," 29 Rec. N.Y.C.B. Ass'n 320 (1974)

Greenya, "Public Interest Lives! And Here's Who's Doing It," 8 Dist. Lawyer 32 (1984)

Gunther, *Cases and Materials on Constitutional Law* (1975)

132

Hall, "Public Interest by the Numbers," 31 Stan. L. Rev. 989 (1979)

Halpern, "Public Interest Law: Its Past and Future," 58 Judicature 118 (1974)

Handler, *Social Movement & the Legal System: A Theory of Law and Social Change* (1978)

Handler, Hollingsworth, Erlanger & Ladinsky, "The Public Interest Activities of Private Practice Lawyers," 61 A.B.A.J. 1388 (1975)

Havemann, "New Senate Difficulty Besets Regulatory Review Office," *Wash. Post,* August 16, 1986 at A8 col. 1

Heineman, "In Pursuit of Public Interest Law," 84 Yale L.J. 182 (1974)

Herman and Hoffman, "Financing Public Interest Litigation in State Court," 63 Cornell L. Rev. 173 (1978)

Horowitz, *The Courts and Social Policy* (1977)

Houck, "With Charity for All," 93 Yale L.J. 1415 (1984)

Johnson, *Justice and Reform: The Formative Years of the OEO Legal Services Program* (1974)

Kamp, "The Multistate Consumer Class Action: Local Solutions, National Problems," 87 W. Va. L. Rev. 271 (1985)

Katz, *Poor People's Lawyers in Transition* (1982)

Kerlow, "Hirschkop the Horrible: A '60s Lawyer in the '80s," 9 *Legal Times* 2 (July 21, 1986)

Kinoy, *Rights on Trial* (1980)

Lawyer's Committee for Civil Rights Under Law, *Ten Year Report* (1973)

Lawyer's Committee for Civil Rights Under Law, *Fifteenth Anniversary Report* (1978)

Lawyer's Committee for Civil Rights Under Law, *Annual Report 1985-1986*

Lee, "Pro Bono Profile: People Want to do Something," 10 Barrister 29 (Fall 1983)

Legal Services Corporation, *Annual Report for Fiscal Years 1982 and 1983*

Lewin & Steiger, *To Light One Candle: A Handbook for Organizing, Funding and Maintaining Public Service Activities* (1978)

Lewin, "The Fast Track: Leaving the Law for Wall Street," N.Y. Times Magazine, section 6 at 14 (August 10, 1986)

Marcus, "Persistent Lawyer Makes Burger Recant," *Wash. Post,* August 10, 1986 at A6 col. 1

Marshall, "Financing Public Interest Law Practice: The Role of the Organized Bar," 61 A.B.A.J. 1487 (1975)

133

McKay, "Civil Litigation in the Public Interest," 31 U. Kan. L. Rev. 355 (1983)

Mezey, "Judicial Interpretation of Legislative Intent: The Role of the Supreme Court in the Implication of Private Rights of Action," 36 Rutgers L. Rev. 53 (1983)

Milstein, "How Public Advocates Made Poverty Law (Almost) Profitable," 5 Am. Lawyer 77 (December 1983)

Moore, *Moore's Federal Practice* (1979 with 1986 supp.)

Myers, "Standing in Public Interest Litigation: Removing the Procedural Barriers," 15 Loyola L.A. L. Rev. 1 (1981)

Nadar and Green, *Verdicts on Lawyers* (1976)

Nadar and Schultz, "Public Interest Law With Bread on the Table," 71 A.B.A. J. 74 (1985)

National Association for the Advancement of Colored People, Legal Defense and Education Fund, *Annual Reports for the Years 1982-1983, 1983-1984, 1984-1985, and 1985-1986*

National Association for the Advancement of Colored People, Legal Defense and Education Fund, *Brown v. Board of Education—Thirty Years Later: "The Politics of Experience"* (1983)

National Lawyers Guild, *Organizational Report,* (January 1986)

Note, "Award of Attorney's Fees to Unsuccessful Environmental Litigants," 96 Harv. L. Rev. 677 (1983)

Note, "Challenge of the New Lawyers: Public Interest and Private Clients," 38 Geo. Wash. L. Rev. 527 (1970)

Note, "The New Public Interest Lawyers," 79 Yale L.J. 1069 (1970)

Note, "Structuring the Public Service Efforts of Private Law Firms," 84 Harv. L. Rev. 410 (1970)

O'Connor and Epstein, "Rebalancing the Scales of Justice: Assessment of Public Interest Law," 7 Harv. J. L. & Pub. Pol'y 483 (1984)

Pendlebury, "Associate Salary Wars: Branch Offices Leave D.C. Firms in Dust," 9 *Legal Times* 1 (September 1, 1986)

Pertschuk, *Giant Killers?* (1986)

Popeo, "Public Interest Law in the 1980s," *Barron's* (March 2, 1981)

Public Citizen, "1984: The Year in Review," Public Citizen Mag., (Spring 1985)

Public Citizen, "The Year in Review," Public Citizen Mag., (April 1986)

Public Citizen, "Car Dealers Gave $1/2 Million to Co-Sponsors of Car Dealers' Relief Bill, Nader Group Finds," Press Release (November 1981)

Public Citizen Litigation Group, "1985 Public Citizen Litigation Group Activities," Press Release (January 1986)

Rabin, "Lawyers for Social Change: Perspectives in Public Interest Law," 28 Stan. L. Rev. 207 (1976)

Rabkin, "Public Interest Law: Is it Law in the 'Public Interest'?," 8 Harv. J. L. & Pub. Pol'y 341 (1983)

Rivlin, "A Break from the Past (Cooperation Between Legal Services Attorneys and Private Bar in Central Mississippi Legal Services Program)," 69 A.B.A.J. 178 (1983)

Roberts, "The Art of Public Interest Lobbying," *N. Y. Times,* January 2, 1986

Romfeldt, "Implying Rights of Action for Minorities and the Poor Through Presumptions of Legislative Intent," 34 Hastings L. J. 969 (1983)

Rust, "What Pro Bono Can't Do," 13 Stud. Lawyer 25 (1985)

Saltzman, "Private Bar Delivery of Civil Legal Services to the Poor: A Design for a Combined Private Attorney and Staffed Office Delivery System," 34 Hastings L. J. 1165 (1983)

Schwartz, "Federal Practice Notes: Attorneys' Fees Developments," 19 Clearinghouse Rev. 36 (May 1985)

Searcy, "Marketing the Public Interest," 9 Pipeline 1 (Spring 1986)

Seymour, *Why Justice Fails* (1973)

Smith, *Justice and the Poor* (1919)

Stern, *Lawyers on Trial,* (1980)

Stille, "Seeking Shelter in the Law," 8 Nat'l L. J. 1 (February 10, 1986)

Stover, "The Importance of Economic Supply in Determining the Size and Quality of the Public Interest Bar," 16 Law & Soc'y Rev. 455 (1982)

Stresser and Effron, "The Bar's Voice?," 9 Nat'l L. J. 49 (August 18, 1986)

Taylor, "Legal Aid for the Poor Did Work and That's the Problem," *N. Y. Times* section E at 3 col. 1 (March 15, 1981)

Teitelman, "The Ethical Responsibility to Provide Free Legal Services," 7 Wash. U. L. Sch. Mag. 13 (1985)

Trial Lawyers for Public Justice, *Annual Report 1985*

Tribe, *Constitutional Law* (1979)

Tucker, *"Pro Bono Publico* or *Pro Bono* Organized Bar?," 60 A.B.A. J. 914 (1974)

Turner, "Federal Jurisdiction after *Pennhurst,"* 4 Calif. Lawyer 10 (September 1984)

135

Weisbroad, *Public Interest Law: An Economic and Institutional Analysis* (1978)

Wright and Miller, *Federal Practice and Procedure* (1973 with 1986 supp.)

———, "Supreme Court Review," 8 Nat'l L.J. S-1 (August 11, 1986)

———, "Supreme Court Review: The Gavel Passes," 8 Nat'l L.J. 15 (June 30, 1986)

INDEX

138